WE ARE CALLED TO BE

COMPANIONS
—— *of the* ——
CROSS

Also by Fr. Bob Bedard, CC

Give God Permission
The Memoirs of Fr. Bob Bedard, CC

The Catholic Disciple

Evangelization
A Challenge for the Catholic Church

WE ARE CALLED TO BE

COMPANIONS
—— *of the* ——
CROSS

Insights and Reflections
on Our Life in Christ

Fr. Bob Bedard, CC
Founder of the Companions of the Cross

Published by
COMPANIONS OF THE CROSS
Ottawa, Ontario, Canada

COMPANIONS OF THE CROSS

199 Bayswater Avenue
Ottawa, Ontario K1Y 2G5

www.companionscross.org

WE ARE CALLED TO BE COMPANIONS *of the* CROSS
Insights and Reflections on Our Life in Christ
by Fr. Bob Bedard, CC
© 1994, 2013 Companions of the Cross. All rights reserved.

Printed in Ottawa, Canada
No part of this work may be reproduced, stored in a retrieval system or transmitted in any form or by any means, electronic, mechanical, or otherwise, without express written permission.
Nihil Obstat: Richard Jaworski, CC, S.S.L., Vice-Moderator
Imprimatur: Terrance Prendergast, SJ, D.D., Archbishop of Ottawa
September 14, 2013

Second Edition

ISBN 9781686163043

Cover Art: *The Crucifixion of Jesus Christ (John 3:16)* by William J. Wallace, 1979.
Artist Description: This painting was finished by Bill Wallace after 3 years of research and work. It is also called *John 3:16* as it depicts humanity; the "whosoever's" from all walks of life throughout history. Many stories are depicted within the painting which reinforces the desire of the Father's heart, that no one perish, but everyone to come to repentance and be saved through his son Jesus Christ. (John 3:16, II Peter 3:9)

Contents

Introduction by Bishop Scott McCaig, CC IX
Fr. Bob's Introduction XIII

**1 RESPONDING TO THE
    CURRENT STATE OF THINGS** 1
    What We're Up Against 1
    Magisterium 12
    Scripture, Tradition and Magisterium 13
    A Modern Challenge 15
    Where We Stand 17
    The Renewal of a Parish 21
    Crisis in Masculinity 32

2 STRATEGIES FOR TODAY'S CHURCH 37
    The Renewal of the Mind 37
    Baptised with the Spirit 40
    Gifts of the Holy Spirit 43
    Wisdom 48
    Ministry 54
    Evangelization 58
    Ministry Hazards 63

3 GROWING INTO DISCIPLESHIP — 67
Repentance — 68
Praise — 71
Prayer — 74
Obedience — 79
Fasting — 82
Journaling — 85
Feelings and Discernment — 86
Simplicity of Life — 89
Tithing — 97
Handling Adversity — 100

4 SUPPORTING ONE ANOTHER — 107
Loving One Another — 107
Affirmation — 111
Unity — 113
Reconciling with One Another — 116

5 COMPANIONS OF THE CROSS — 119
Background — 119
A Short History — 120
The Priesthood — 127
Celibacy — 132
The Cross — 135
Basic Components of the Vision — 137
Spirituality — 142
How we pray — 143
How we live together — 144
How we work — 144
Life Together — 146
Positional Statement — 149
The Lay Associates — 152
Living out the Commitment — 155

6 MARY, THE FIRST COMPANION OF THE CROSS ... 161
That all may be one ... 161
Model ... 163
Highly favoured daughter ... 165
Minister ... 165
Presentation ... 166
God's agents ... 168
Music and Incense ... 169
Cana ... 171
The Hour Arrives ... 173
This is your mother ... 175
The dialogue ... 176
The brothers and sisters ... 179
Magnificat ... 181
Dogmas ... 181
A Prophet for today ... 184
A gift from God ... 185

Introduction by Fr. Scott McCaig, CC

INTRODUCTION

"The last thing the Church needs is another community. We need about half the ones we already have." This is a quote from the early musings of Fr. Bob Bedard. As he was so fond of saying, they soon fell into the category of famous last words!

In addition to being a true pioneer of the 'New Evangelization' and the 'New Pentecost' in our time, he became Founder of the Companions of the Cross—a community of priests dedicated to the renewal of the Church through a dynamic evangelization in the power of the Holy Spirit. He also inspired the formation of an associated sisterhood and a lay association for those who felt called to embrace our spirituality and mission. To all of us who embraced the vision that God had placed in his heart, he became our spiritual father in Christ.

Father Bob passed away on October 6, 2011, but he continues to teach and inspire us through the many newsletter articles he left us, his recorded homilies and talks, and the handful of books he wrote. The volume before you is part of that treasured legacy.

The first brothers were formed in the vision of life, spirituality, and mission that the Lord had fashioned in Fr. Bob's heart over many years. Father Bob drew from his own experiences of common life, the insights that the Lord was giving to the young community, and from the homilies and talks he had given at various conferences and prayer groups in the 1970's and 1980's. Eventually he was persuaded to bring a number of these teachings together into a single volume, not only for the community but for anyone who might be interested. The first edition of *We are Called to be Companions of the Cross* was published in 1994. For many years it served as the principle formation manual and repository of the 'vision' of the community.

Eventually, as the community continued to grow and develop, so too did our understanding of the vision. Today we are guided by our Constitutions and Rules and by a greatly expanded formation program. But this book is still at the heart of all that we are about. It contains many of the core inspirations and convictions that have directed the community from the beginning. One could almost say that this little book represents the seed from which the community grew.

Some of this material may seem dated. Various statistics that are cited may no longer be accurate. And portions of this material were later modified in some of Fr. Bob's subsequent works. But apart from removing a few redundancies and a few chapters that described canonical matters that no longer apply, we have left it unchanged. We have done so not only because it is an important part of our spiritual patrimony, but also because it is a compelling work. Rereading it again after so many years only confirms how prophetic Fr. Bob truly was! The examples may be dated, but this work is as relevant as it ever was.

It is our fervent hope that you will be inspired by the clarity, fervour, and insight of Fr. Bob. For those who knew and loved him it will be an opportunity to be stirred again by this priest after God's own heart. For those who are new to Fr. Bob and the Companions of the Cross we pray that his wisdom will lead you to a deeper following of the Lord.

To all we pray for God's richest blessings and a fresh outpouring of the fire of the Holy Spirit.

> Fr. Scott McCaig, CC
> Feast of the Exaltation of the Holy Cross, September 14, 2013.

> *Fr. Scott McCaig, CC served as General Superior of the Companions of the Cross from 2006-2016. He was ordained to the Episcopate on May 31, 2016. He now serves as Bishop of the Roman Catholic Military Ordinariate of Canada.*

FR. BOB'S INTRODUCTION

The writings in this collection were intended originally for the Companions of the Cross, the community of priests and candidates for the priesthood and consecrated brotherhood that the Lord seems to have some of us in the process of founding. I suppose that is what, primarily, they still are.

But, once they were in readable form, people began telling us that perhaps we should consider making them available to a wider readership. This has been an unexpected development. But that has become standard experience for us now.

It has taken me a while to catch on, but I think I finally have got it straight now: God consistently does unexpected things.

Reading the Scriptures should have convinced me of it long ago, but, unless we experience something ourselves, I guess it is difficult for us really to believe that what we read there represents an actual pattern for the present. It came home to me clearly one day at Mass when both the first and second readings reported the unexpected.

The first Scripture was from the Old Testament Book of Jonah—full of surprises. Jonah, the reluctant prophet, was a most unlikely prospect for the daunting enterprise God had in mind: nothing less than the total conversion of the pagan metropolis of Nineveh. When, under protest and without a great measure of enthusiasm, Jonah finally did the Lord's bidding, it worked. In spite of his limitations, God worked through him. Nineveh was converted and spared the fate toward which it was surely headed. Amazing. Quite unexpected.

The Gospel was taken from St. Luke's tenth chapter. In the scene at Bethany that he describes, Martha, overburdened and obviously frustrated, suggests to Jesus that he send her sister, Mary, who was doing nothing more than just sitting and listening to him, to help with the work. With Martha, I would have anticipated a favourable response from Jesus: that he would tell Mary to hop to it. (Mary of Bethany was no favourite, incidentally, of my mother, who said more than once: "I don't care what anybody says. That Mary was nothing but a lazy lump.") But Jesus did not see it Martha's way. He affirmed what Mary was doing. Again, the unexpected.

But the Lord is like that. He is continually doing things we are not anticipating at all. Can we hear him saying: *"My ways are not your ways. As high as the sky is above the earth, so high are my ways above your ways"* (Isa 55:8-9)?

I consider this community, the Companions of the Cross, to be one of God's surprises. Nobody foresaw it. We did not plan it or prepare for it in any way. It was as though we were moving toward it without knowing where we were going. All of a sudden, it seemed, in the spring of 1985, there we were. When, a few months later, the Archbishop confirmed the vision, we were sure the Lord had actually spoken.

And the unexpected did not end there. Surprising things have continued to occur. We felt that God might have been telling us that, if we embraced the vision we thought he was giving us, he would prosper it and quickly add to our number. This seemed, to say the least, unlikely. For we had been meeting for almost a year and a half and had grown only from four to five. Yet, within a few weeks, 15 men were meeting to explore the possibility of becoming part of the community. The Lord of surprises? I'll say! I am starting to get used to it now. The only thing is—I never know what's going to happen next. I never know if the 'word' we think we are hearing is authentic until it actually happens. Because we can get it wrong. I have a long history of that myself. Lots of precedent. I have, of course, learned, in the process, not to take myself too seriously.

The Lord gives his vision, I am convinced, to those who seek it and pledge themselves to follow it, but he does not seem to provide a full blueprint. He does not lay out flow charts and timetables for us. There is much that will continue to remain unclear.

That, too, is part of his plan, his overall strategy. Not knowing everything draws us to trust him. Trusting in God is not a gift. It is a decision. Like getting up in the morning.

While I place all my trust in God, I still, nonetheless, have questions. I wonder, for example, how we will be able to support all the 'brothers' and provide them with places to live. We have never had much money. We have always financed very close to the line. We have never had to wonder where to invest what was left over.

But...we believe the Lord will supply. He always has. What he authorizes, he underwrites.

It is all quite an adventure. Sometimes I think I am getting too old for it, but I've decided to stay in it for the long haul anyway. It will probably, better than anything else, keep me young. Trying to run with the Lord of the unexpected is very exciting. Breathtaking, in fact.

If reading about the Companions of the Cross and being exposed to the basic teachings we believe the Lord has given us can be a source of blessing to even a few people, we will be truly grateful.

CHAPTER ONE

Responding to the Current State of Things

What We're Up Against
The development of nuclear arms makes this age of world history unique. There has never been a time quite like this one. We have never before had the capacity, as a human race, to annihilate ourselves completely. The prospect is so horrible that we tend to deal with the issue basically by ignoring it. Who can blame us? Who wants to spend time thinking about things like that?

Some years ago, as I read somewhere, a commentator was explaining that we had, at that time, enough nuclear explosives to kill everybody on earth 20 times. Not only that, we were continuing to manufacture additional weapons. And the new weaponry would have more and more effective capacity for destruction. There is, of course, an obvious insanity about it all.

Not so long ago, the 'nuclear club', as it is euphemistically referred to, had nine member countries, nine nations that possessed nuclear capacity. But, we are told, the club is expanding all the time. Before long, predictions are, upwards of 20 countries will have the same capacity.

The proliferation of such weapons, we must know, makes it more and more likely that somebody, somewhere, sometime will use them. Can we see a dispute breaking out between smaller nations, neither of which has much by way of conventional arms, including the possibility, even though limited, of a nuclear 'exchange' (another euphemism).

Never in the history of the world has a nation manufactured arms without using them. We don't like to think that this will happen with the nuclear weapons, but we have to be realistic.

It could well happen.

The present (1990) breakdown of communism in Eastern Europe has had the understandable effect of giving many of us a real hope of finding our way out, after all, of what had been looking like a hopeless impasse.

Nonetheless, the nuclear factor alone serves to make living in these times somewhat precarious. Those of us who are charged by the Lord with proclaiming the Gospel must take it into account that those to whom we witness know, if only in their subconscious, that they are living continually on the brink of disaster.

In addition, we live in a world that takes economic imbalance for granted. The gap between the rich and the poor nations, the north and the south, as some term it, is ever widening, even day by day.

We have literally attacked the environment that the Lord has provided for us, done it violence, and placed it in jeopardy. All this to secure for the upper strata of human society a standard of living that God probably never intended. It is very nice to have it, but the problem with it is that, in order for the few to enjoy it, the great majority must content themselves with living in circumstances that only inadequately serve their needs.

We have wrested from the earth the resources needed to keep the wealthy at the level they have come to need. We have bent the environment to our purposes. A few years ago, one report had it that 86% of the world's natural resources were being deployed to provide what 14% of the world's population wanted. The writer went on to explain that, as time went on, a greater and greater percentage of the resources would be needed for a smaller and smaller percentage of the people. The reality is that capital controls resources.

Maintaining these living standards (the ideal is living on the isolated large estate) has necessitated transferring resources from one set of nations to another, from the poorer to the richer. It has required keeping a large number of the world's nations and their people, the so-called 'third world', in grinding poverty. Its inhabitants must work for a pittance so that the people in the 'first world' can continue to live the way they do, and, not only that, but be able to look forward to better and better standards.

The nations of the third world are required to be suppliers of resources to their developed neighbours who, in turn, will take some of the resources, manufacture goods from them, and sell them back to the supplier countries. This all helps to keep the countries of the south, as they are sometimes called, into everspiralling levels of debt. This is not only unjust. It is dangerous.

The time will surely come when some of the hopelessly debtridden nations will begin to default on their payments. Their creditors, large lending houses in the richer nations, could then start to feel the pinch themselves. Can we imagine what would happen if some of our most trusted and solid financial institutions began to go under? The economies of the first world could be thrown into chaos and lead to a series of events which would force us all back to realistic living standards.

The keeping of the citizens of the disadvantaged nations at mere subsistence levels has, of course, opened the doors for the preaching of another gospel, the gospel of Karl Marx. To make the point that the rich continue to live in luxury on the backs of the poor is pretty persuasive rhetoric. Communism has grown at an amazing pace. And, although it has recently been losing its hold on Europe, it is, nonetheless, strong, and getting stronger, in the developing nations. It has been creating a whole, huge 'second world'. The sight of comfortable Christians in the richer nations, people who will not sacrifice their high standards of living for the sake of justice, does not lend a lot of authenticity to our witness.

The Church's social gospel is clear. Prophetic statement after prophetic statement has issued from the highest levels of our Church for over a century. But they have been slow to catch on with the faithful. We have yet to develop a workable alternative to the capitalist and communist systems. We know the exploitation of the masses has to stop. We just don't seem to have reached yet that point of conversion at which we will actually do the things needed to stop it.

Most of the systems in the free world have embraced some level of unemployment as an economic necessity. We have developed a whole network of welfare payments to keep the unemployed at a barely adequate lifestyle. This may serve to keep the system going, but it robs people of their human dignity, keeps them basically idle, and opens them up to being victimized by their own weaknesses. People are driven into chemical and alcohol abuse, promiscuity, violence, and crime. Life can become a battleground where battered women and abused children are commonplace. Those who are chronically unemployed become incredibly wounded in their inner beings and develop very bad self-images. Enforced poverty can take hold of whole families and can become an affliction that takes generations to heal. Trying to bring the Gospel into lives so brutalized can be a daunting task indeed.

Into the struggle between big government and big business has, in our day, entered a new combatant—big labour. We live, whether we like it or not, in a 'strike' culture. Any group that wants more simply withdraws services. We all become tainted, as we manoeuver to maintain or better our positions, with the greed syndrome.

We who preach the Gospel of the Lord have to call people, including ourselves, to a much simpler lifestyle. We have to call for a spirit of real sacrifice and an end to greed. But we have to know that we will not be very popular if we do.

Along with the woes described, there is arising a crisis in public morality. We have seen, in little more than a generation, a distressing breakdown in the institution of marriage, once regarded as one of society's basic institutions. It is no longer unusual for spouses, having lived together for 10, 20, 30 years or more, to announce that they are calling it quits. We are not scandalized any more, it seems, when a very prominent federal member of parliament, questioned about the live-in arrangement he has with his girl friend, his wife having departed the scene, says: "What's the matter with it? After all, this is not the 19th century. We are living in a more enlightened time, surely."

It doesn't seem to bother us much, either, when an enormously popular athlete, one who is routinely touted as an excellent model for our youth, goes to the altar to be married to his already pregnant fiancée. If we raise our eyebrows at such things, we will certainly be told that these are the 1990's. Sexual mores have changed and, it seems, will continue to do so. Cohabitation before marriage has become the norm. More than one pastor has reported that almost 80% of couples presenting themselves for matrimonial preparation in the last while are already living together.

In the current scare about the dreaded AIDS virus, sociologists and educational authorities are promoting something called 'safe sex'. All, including youngsters, are urged to carry condoms around with them in purses and wallets. High schools are giving them out. It doesn't seem to be occurring to too many that the only real way to avoid infection is God's way, abstinence before marriage and fidelity within. We would be laughed out of any public meeting for suggesting it.

The assault on the unborn continues and escalates. We live in a country with, at this writing, no abortion law at all. It is open season on the unborn. The most dangerous place to live anywhere in our society has become a mother's womb.

In the political realm, dishonesty is taken for granted. It is now routine in our country in the days and months after an election for several ministers of the crown to have to resign for one monetary scandal or another. It is almost as though we have returned to the ancient spoils-of-office system.

We are paying the price for all this. We are seeing an alarming increase in violent crime, child abuse, addiction to alcohol and drugs, social disease, and suicide.

It is my impression that the so-called age of enlightenment has come to an end. Its reasoned solutions to our problems have not worked, and we have become very disillusioned. We have lost confidence in ourselves, in our capacity to find ways to deal with the dilemma we find ourselves in. Many have turned to bizarre alternatives. There is an alarming increase in occult activity. Satanic groups have multiplied. Witches' covens have appeared in unexpected places. There is fascination with the spiritualities of the East. And there is a whole conglomeration of programs and techniques that open people up to spiritual interference, all going by the now generic phrase 'New Age'.

There is a spirit of rebellion abroad in the land. The members of the 'me generation' are intent on doing their own thing and will brook no attempts to restrain them.

How have we got ourselves into such a mess? It has been caused by the very thing that Jesus came to save us from—sin. We have, as a human race, rebelled against God. We have taken control of creation and turned it to our own purposes. The weight of sin upon the world has piled up to the point that it is causing the structures under which we live to crack and even collapse. God is allowing us to experience the consequences of our own decisions.

How heavy is the weight of sin today? A couple of years ago, I heard a priest I respect very much say that it is its heaviest in history. Having taught ancient and mediaeval history in high school, I was remembering tales of societies more corrupt even than our own, and I was having trouble understanding how the weight of sin today could be heavier than in some of those. And yet, somehow, I felt he was right. It came clear to me when he reminded us that the population of today's world equals the total populations of all past ages. It is the multiplication of sin that is causing its incredible weight.

Some tend to minimize the concern I believe we should have about all this by saying that it's just a matter of cycles. Sure, they say, things aren't too great these days, but we'll bounce back. We always have. There are brighter days ahead. Not to worry.

I believe there are brighter days ahead, but I think, at the same time, that we are in a deteriorating situation from which we may not just bounce back before collapsing altogether. My feeling is that there is a breaking point, and that we're getting there fast. The moral collapse may get worse and portend economic, political, and military crises. There is even, I'm afraid, the possibility that nature itself may rise up in rebellion against us who have, in our turn, rebelled against God. Natural disasters could escalate.

All in all, this a very bleak picture painted by a very hopeful and naturally optimistic guy. Not everybody will agree with my assessment at this point. Nonetheless, I am filled with hope and believe we should look to the future with great anticipation.

God is going to turn things around.

Ordinarily, he would have done this long ago through the Church had we, as his people, had our act more together than we have.

The Church is meant by the Lord to be the leaven in society (Matt 13:33). Unfortunately, the leaven has just not been working. The Church is intended to have the power to change the world. But we don't seem to be plugged in to the power source. Rather, in some places at least, the Church is with the world, on the ropes.

Here, in our part of the world, the Church has come upon lean times. There has been a striking decline in what we call the 'practice' of the faith. Every new set of statistics, every poll taken, brings us the distressing news that fewer and fewer Catholics are attending church on a regular basis. The numbers are not encouraging.

There is a dearth of vocations to the priesthood and religious life, with some communities in danger of disappearing altogether within the next generation. There are some noteworthy exceptions to this seeming norm, but it is difficult to know what the Lord's strategy is. Does he intend to renew the structures we have, or has he in mind to replace them completely? It seems at least plain that those bodies not open to radical renewal will disappear.

We have been experiencing, too, a revolt of the academics within the Church. Too many of our theologians and Scripture scholars have been developing a new agenda for the Church, teaching things that directly contradict the official Magisterium. We are hearing that Jesus didn't really rise from the dead, that there is no actual original sin to be saved from, that Jesus didn't found the Church as we have it today, that the concept of hierarchy is manmade, that the ordained priesthood is not qualitatively different from the priesthood of all the faithful, that Jesus is not really present in the Eucharist, that we need to revise our moral laws, and many other like things. It is difficult to refrain from comparing the present state of much of our theology to the situation St. Paul was addressing when he wrote to the Romans. Some have, he said, *"exchanged the truth of God for a lie"* (Rom 1:25).

These academic developments have affected many of our Catholic institutions of higher learning, including some of our seminaries. Since, as we believe, the renewal of the

Church is to begin with the renewal of the priesthood, it is not difficult to see what a problem this poses.

It has been said that we are heading for a schism, that there is, in fact, a de facto schism in the North American Church right now, and that proponents of the new agenda for God's people will end by taking great numbers of Catholics outside the Church. This seems unlikely. Many of the said academics, when asked why they do not leave the Church since they disagree with so many of the things it stands for, reply that they have no intention of leaving. They intend, they say, to remain with the Church and change it from within. Even if they did defect, it might not be called schism. Not so long ago, I asked Archbishop Ambrozic, co-adjutor of Toronto, what he thought about it. "It would not be a schism," he said. "To qualify as a schism, they would have to have faith. There is no faith there. It is a crisis of faith we're looking at."

There are numerous well-organized lobbies within the Church, some of which have become very influential, particularly in our own country. The feminist lobby would be the most powerful of these. The liberationist and gay advocacy movements are likewise significant. And there are others. For the most part, they seem to be mainly secular humanist in their goals and intent upon creating a heaven on earth. They are much like religion without the participation of God. The Church has become for them a useful vehicle, a way to realize their goals.

How has all this come to happen? There is a factor, I am convinced, that we do not recognize too well or understand. It is the reality of spiritual war. The fact of the matter is that Satan has stepped up the intensity of the battle several notches in our time. One Christian writer has said, correctly I think: "You simply cannot imagine the ferocity of the battle that is being waged around you." It is a battle for the soul of man and it is directed at the human mind. The assault on young people is particularly intense. The whole field of entertainment has been infected. The movies, the videos, the music, all aimed at youth especially, are promoting values that do not come from God.

I won't help my own credibility rating when I suggest that there may be an unseen hand calling a lot of the shots. We may be looking at a very careful engineering job and a grand-scale deception (we are not immune to deception) of incredible proportions.

We can certainly take consolation from the official Magisterium of the Church. The response from the highest levels of leadership within the Church is consistently right-on. If we want to know where we're at and where we're to go, we can do no better than to hearken carefully to the Pope and the bishops.

But the Church at large is asleep. Most of us have been lulled into basic inactivity and cling to a rather vague hope that somehow things are bound eventually to improve. Significant segments of the Church are paralysed by a false optimism. Because we think things will be okay, we're doing nothing. Because most of our churches are surviving and not closing, because there are some good programs coming out, because we have Catholic schools, because Mass is still being said and sacraments are being dispensed, too many heads are in the sand. We are satisfied with a pastoral strategy that is limited to providing religious services to support people on their way to heaven.

There is large-scale denial among us of the reality of the spiritual war. Whatever the Church teaches us officially, in practice most of us just don't believe Satan exists or that there is a battle to worry about at all. Because of this, we are ill-equipped to fight the war. And many are getting wiped out. As one teacher put it a couple of years ago: "If you don't know you're in a war, you're already losing." The enemy is wreaking devastation on our marriages and on our children, and we are standing by wondering why it is happening. We are not armed for the contest. We are like children ourselves, going out into a battle with only pea-shooters and water pistols to defend ourselves against the enemy's tank corps.

And when some among us begin to perceive the extent of the crisis we face, there is too much reliance on merely human efforts and programs to combat it.

Where does it all leave us? We, the Companions of the Cross, are but a drop in the bucket in the whole Church scene. We kid ourselves if we think we can wade into the fight and do big damage to the enemy. We are not going to scare anybody. But that, of course, is not the point. We are not to be concerned with being effective. We are to be faithful, faithful simply to what the Lord has called us to be. What he may want to accomplish through us is his business and known only to him.

On our part, we must open up to the truth that God himself wants to direct the Church and every component within it, including us. The answer, we know, is Jesus himself, and the wisdom and power of his Holy Spirit.

We know that God is not idle. We know that he has launched an initiative of his own. He has been making available that peculiar grace called the baptism of the Spirit, a grace that has the potential to capture the hearts of men and women and set them on fire for the kingdom of God. What we have to do is go along with what God himself is doing. He is recruiting people in every part of the world, all those who are ready to abandon themselves to his purposes, and he is preparing them to work with him for a powerful renewal of his Church.

Numbers are not significant, not with the Lord. He has always been able to do a lot with a little. The Bible is full of examples. He was able to use Gideon and his 300 to defeat an opponent thousands strong. A remnant is all he needs. We have to choose to be part of the remnant.

The Lord has great plans, far greater than we can imagine. His purpose in our day is, I believe, nothing short of the renewal of the entire Church, including its reunification. A large order? Not for God. He has already released the grace that can make it happen.

He has sent a herald to announce his plans. She is Mary, the mother of Jesus. The last 150 years have seen her appear again and again to prophesy to the Church. Although only a few of the hundreds of reported apparitions have been authenticated by the Church, in these she has made it plain that God intends to bring his people through. 'An era of peace' is the way she put it at Fatima. The necessary grace has now been made available. She is the herald of that grace.

One of the priests of this local Church, Fr. Joe Muldoon, currently pastor of St. Maurice's parish, says he believes God intends to change the course of human history and that he has already begun. He further believes it is going to involve a thorough shake-down of the Church, not just a few cosmetic adjustments.

Will there be a total economic collapse world-wide? Will we have to suffer through disastrous earthquakes, hurricanes, typhoons, and droughts? Will we have to dig ourselves out after a nuclear holocaust? We don't have answers to these questions. We can certainly hope and pray that the Lord will spare us from such things.

Right now, the Companions of the Cross are a group of men gathered around a vision that is in the process of taking place. Not much of real significance has yet happened. Very few structures are in place. What the Lord wants, I believe, is for those of us who will, to commit ourselves without reserve to him, without reserve to one another, and without reserve to what he has asked us to be and to do. If enough of us will do this, I think he has been telling us, he will be able to make happen with us what he wants to make happen.

What are we up against? We are up against plenty. But it is no time to be faint-hearted. It is time to be faithful to God.

Magisterium

Jesus Christ, appointed by the Father as head and Shepherd of the Church, promised not to leave us orphans (John 14:8), but to abide with us to the very end of time (Matt 28:20), and to send us *"another Advocate"* (John 14:16), the Holy Spirit, to lead us into the fullness of truth.

The principal way God's Spirit carries this out is through the ministry of the apostles, a ministry established by Christ himself. The apostles and their lawful successors (the bishops) alone possess the charism of authoritative teaching. The 'college' of bishops, united with its head, the bishop of Rome, is the official teaching body within the Church. The Pope is the locus of the Church's teaching authority. He is invested with a special charism, infallibility, in order to enunciate and, when necessary, to solemnly define the universal beliefs of God's faithful and prayerful people. To this college of bishops is given the term 'Magisterium'.

As long as the faithful remain in communion with these shepherds, they cannot err in matters of belief (*Lumen Gentium* 12). "The Catholic Church is, by the will of Christ, the teacher of truth. It is her duty to proclaim and teach with authority the truth which is Christ and, at the same time, to declare and confirm by her authority the principles of the moral order which spring from human nature itself" (*Dignitatis Humanae* 14).

Scripture, Tradition and Magisterium

The Magisterium is not superior to the word of God, but is its servant. The Word of God is the primary norm of faith. God's holy Word has been progressively revealed through salvation history, refined and reaching its completion in the person and teaching of Jesus himself, the very incarnate Word of God. The Lord's revelation has been confided to his people through both the sacred, inspired writings (the Scriptures), and holy Tradition, which is those truths left implicit by Jesus and made explicit by his Church under the guidance of the Holy Spirit (see John 16:12).

This revelation is not only static, however; it is also dynamic and needs interpretation in every age.

At the heart of God's revelation are what we call mysteries, religious truths that can be known only by revelation, and even once revealed can never be exhaustively comprehended. The Church's understanding of these mysteries can develop and mature as God's people make their pilgrim way through history.

The Church's understanding of the Lord's Word is subject to development in this way, and the Church's expression of it is subject to change. This is because the Church's proclamation of the Lord's Word is always formulated in particular historical and cultural contexts, contexts that change.

Among the truths of Catholic doctrine there also "exists a 'hierarchy', since not all these truths are equally connected with the fundamental Christian faith" (*Unitatis Redintegratio* 11).

Finally, the Lord desires to direct his Church, a desire which necessitates and implies an ongoing word from him. Through this direction, it is the Lord himself who teaches us how to apply and live out his revelation in every age. This is a word that needs ongoing discernment for we are not to be taken in by *"the wisdom of the world"* (1 Cor 1:18-25, 2:1-10), but to be guided by the very wisdom of God himself.

Considering all this, it must be unmistakeably clear that "the task of giving an authentic interpretation of the Word of God, whether in its written form or in the form of tradition, has been entrusted to the living teaching office of the Church alone" (*Dei Verbum* 10). In fact, in keeping with God's own design, both Sacred Scripture and Tradition are inseparable from the Magisterium (*Dei Verbum* 10).

The Magisterium naturally calls on the services of theologians and other scholars to carry out its task. As Pope John Paul II has said to theologians, "we all [the Pope and the bishops] need your work, your dedication and the fruits of your reflection. We desire to listen to you and are eager to receive the valued assistance of your responsible scholarship" (O'Collins, *Fundamental Theology*, p. 260). There is much confusion about the roles of the academics today; so let's be unequivocal about it. The various theologians and scholars are the bishops' advisors. They are the researchers and speculators. They are not the teachers. The bishops are the teachers. The ultimate infallible authority in faith and morals rests with the Magisterium. The work of the scholars is intended to contribute to their discernment.

A Modern Challenge

In our day, Magisterium has become the "M" word. It starts conversations. It induces dialogue. Unfortunately, much of the discussion gets rancorous. Epithets fly. It's just one of those words.

There is widespread dispute about the Magisterium's role. In numerous academic circles, dissent from many of the Church's long-standing positions has become almost de rigueur, has even become highly organized.

Vatican II called for a more open dialogue with the modern world, something long overdue. But, alas, the exchange has had an unforseen result. Some of the members of the Catholic world of academe have been "evangelized" by contemporary thought and culture. The very world to which we have been sent to witness the Gospel has in turn captured many of us.

The whole concept of Tradition as a source of authority is being seriously challenged in our day. The subjectivism of the behavioural sciences has been embraced, overturning in the process long-accepted moral standards. Philosophical relativism has fed into a theology of compromise. Structures and institutions have become suspect, including the hierarchy and the Church itself.

A good number of current-day theologians and other scholars find themselves in opposition to the Church's Magisterium. Many believe the Pope and the bishops have lost effective touch with the direction in which the Holy Spirit has been leading the Church. There are calls for a 'New Magisterium', one comprised of the best minds of the modern Church, those academics best qualified to interpret the Gospel to these times. This new body would be conversant with the findings of all the behavioural sciences and the latest in biblical research. We would have a set of principles and teachings more in step with the developments of modern society. We would be a more relevant Church, a Church ready to move forward. The Pope and the bishops could devote their energies to maintaining and governing the Church. Let the "experts" do the teaching.

The promoters of the 'New Magisterium' are not impressed with the present Holy Father, Pope John Paul II. Never mind that he is an accomplished and celebrated academic himself, holding doctorates in both theology and philosophy. They regard him as rigid and unenlightened, a victim of his Polish background. They receive a uniformly good press, have instant access to the media, which makes the impression that their adherents are much more numerous than they actually are

What trends and teachings would some of these scholars have us embrace?

1. Jesus has left the Church to us. We ourselves must direct and manage it.

2. Evangelization is best understood as efforts to change the unjust structures under which people live, not to convert them to our beliefs.

3. The Church must adapt itself to an ever-changing world. We must not alienate people by what we teach.

4. The Eucharist should be seen mainly as the assembly of God's people. We should seek to find Christ in one another, not so much in the elements.

5. Sin is to be understood mainly in social terms, such situations as the arms race, over population, unequal distribution of resources, the trashing of the environment. The solutions are purely political. Our efforts should be directed at influencing effective political decisions.

6. Catholic moral theology should be extensively revised to

be more in touch with contemporary issues. Many present norms should be re-evaluated and overturned.
7. Faith engages us in a search for truth. We must learn to live with much doubt. Doubts are healthy.
8. The miraculous must be interpreted out of the Scriptures by de-mythologizing them. God does not intervene in human affairs by breaking his own laws.
9. The resurrection of Jesus should be understood metaphorically. The disciples did not "see" him after his death. Rather, they experienced him inwardly and were changed in a remarkable fashion.
10. It is best to regard angels and demons as symbolic.

Where We Stand

For what it's worth, our little community of the Companions of the Cross stands in solidarity with the official Magisterium of the Church. We will have no truck or trade with any 'new' Magisterium.

From the earliest beginnings of the community, we have been strongly persuaded that we are to be loyal to the official teaching authority of the Church. Particular fidelity to the Magisterium is in fact one of the foundations of our community. It is written into our constitutions. But this submission is not some kind of blind, unthinking, reactionary stand. Rather it is a free choice based on the common conviction of our Catholic faith. The Magisterium is the Lord's own gift to his Church, a gift that keeps us clear-minded as we attempt to grow into an authentic life in Christ.

We are more than enthused about the recent publication of the *Profession of Faith and Oath of Fidelity* requested of all those who assume an office to be exercised in the name of the Church. We make our own its words.

"With firm faith, I ... believe all that is contained in the Word of God, whether written or handed down in Tradition, which the Church, either in solemn judgement or by its ordinary and universal teaching authority, sets forth for our belief as revealed by God. I also firmly accept and hold each and every thing clearly proposed by the Church concerning its teaching on faith and morals. Moreover, I adhere with religious submission of intellect and will to the teachings which both the Roman Pontiff and the College of bishops enunciate in the exercise of their authentic teaching authority, even if they do not intend to proclaim those teachings by a definitive act."

As for some of the modern trends and teachings mentioned earlier, what is our response?

1. Jesus has not abandoned us, leaving us to direct and manage the Church on our own. Jesus founded the Church and continues to be its head and shepherd (*Lumen Gentium* 5-7). He wants to be consulted and actually run it himself through the Holy Spirit.

2. Evangelization is more than changing unjust structures and social work. Evangelization is the proclamation of the Gospel in such a way as to elicit a positive response from the hearer. It is the Father's express will that all people accept his Son (Matt 17:5, 1 Tim 2:4). Evangelization is the Church's number-one commission from the Lord. As Companions of the Cross we are specifically dedicated to this work, regarding it as almost a particular charism of the community. Nevertheless, we are more than eager to join forces with the general Church in its promotion of justice and peace, to embrace its well articulated teaching on the "preferential option for the poor" (*Instruction on Certain Aspects of Liberation Theology*, Introduction Ch. VI, 5).

3. The Church is not to conform itself to an ever-changing world. The Church must be concerned with continually measuring itself against the revealed word of God.

4. The Eucharist is not merely a gathering in which we find Christ in one another. The Eucharist is the re-presenting of Jesus' sacrifice on the cross. As well as a gathering of God's people in the context of the Pascal meal, it is a true sacrifice. We acknowledge the primacy of the Eucharistic celebration as the principal source of the true Christian spirit, the origin and fulfilment of the worship shown to the Eucharist outside Mass (Eucharisticum 3, e passim) and as the main gathering place for God's people who join together to give him due worship. But, too, the real presence of Jesus in the elements impels us to spend quality time in churches and chapels where the Blessed Sacrament is reserved.

   We even encourage the establishment of perpetual adoration wherever possible.

5. Sin is not to be understood in exclusively social terms. Sin is, at root, very personal. The unjust structures under which much of the world's population lives surely cry to heaven for redress. We must do what we can to help change them while keeping in mind that the surest way to begin such change is to bring people to personal repentance and to accept Jesus for who he is. In this way, the power of God is released in their lives, enabling them to become children of God and to take up causes or social change in the wisdom and power of God's Spirit.

6. We recognize the need for a thorough renewal and restating of Catholic moral principles. We agree with contemporary scholars that these norms need to be more biblically grounded, more Christocentric, more person-oriented. But we stand firmly with the Holy Father when he insists that teachings of the Church on matters like abortion (*Gaudium et Spes* 27, 51; *Declaration on Procured Abortion* 18; *Humanae Vitae* 14), euthanasia (Gaudium et Spes 27; Declaration on Euthanasia 3), adultery (*Persona Humana* 5, 7), fornication (*Persona Humana* 7), homo-

sexual activity (*Persona Humana* 8), and contraception (*Gaudium et Spes* 51, *Humanae Vitae* 14) are not subject to change.

7. Faith is not an endless immersion in doubt. Faith is a gift from God enabling us to assent to his revealed truths. For people of faith, much of the search for truth is over. Jesus said: *"I am the way, the truth, and the life"* (John 14:6).

8. Biblical miracles are not to be rejected and completely demythologized. Miracles did, and still do, happen. God is always present to us and is at perfect liberty to set aside his "laws" for his own purposes.

9. The resurrection of the Lord should not be understood metaphorically. We hold fast to the resurrection of Jesus from the grave, not as a resuscitation of the flesh but as a transformation into glory. Through his victory over sin and death, we anticipate joining him in this same glory when he comes again.

10. Angels and demons are not imaginative expressions. We believe in the angelic realm of creation, the rebellion of some of the angels under Satan, the prince of darkness, and the reality of the spiritual battle that goes on continually around us.

Furthermore, on issues such as women's ordination, on which the Church has spoke definitively in recent years, the Companions of the Cross will be loyal to, and not question, the decisions taken by the Magisterium.

The Church may not be perfect. That's the human element. It may be struggling, but it has the potential to be the remnant that the Lord will use to touch this hurting world and make significant inroads for the kingdom of God.

We believe the Lord intends to revitalize his Church and that he will build with those who are faithful to him and to the deposit of faith the Magisterium has been guarding and proclaiming all along.

The Church may be scarred and beaten up. But it's going somewhere. It is not the Catholic Historical Society. It is the Church of the living God.

The Renewal of a Parish

The Companions of the Cross are to be, we believe, a community involved in active ministry. While our life together is to come first, and we are to invest a great deal of ourselves in helping the Lord to make it work, the ministry that flows out of it will be an essential part of who we are.

One of the key ministries that we see ourselves carrying out is pastoring parishes, mostly in the central core areas of our cities, to authentic revival in the Holy Spirit.

Much of what is to be shared here is personal testimony, but not so much as it relates to me. Rather, the point in telling all this is to lay out for us the possible blueprint that the Lord wants to use in seeing parishes come alive in genuine renewal.

The suggestion here is not that we have discovered some magic formula that is bound to work, nor that the Lord's intention would be to do the identical thing in every parish. But we think it is possible for us to identify some principles underlying the experiences we have had that can serve to give us some direction. God doesn't want us to re-invent the wheel every time we begin something new. One of the ways to catch the Lord's word for now is to look backwards and see what he has already obviously said and done.

I had spent 19 years of my priesthood teaching in high school before moving into full-time renewal work. Although I had helped out in parishes all this time, I had never been pastor. In fact, I had avoided it as best I could, making other suggestions to the archbishop every time he mentioned to me the possibility of my becoming a parish priest. I just didn't have the heart for the task, as I used to say. For some reason, I couldn't see myself doing it.

In the summer of 1984, I had what I considered to be a

unique opportunity. I was invited to speak at three different conferences in Canada, one in the west, one in the east, and one in the central part of the country. Since the themes of the three gatherings were very similar, I gave virtually the same talk at each. I felt the word I was supposed to deliver concerned parish renewal. I tried to make the point that, if the Lord's underlying purpose in releasing this peculiar grace known commonly as baptism in the Holy Spirit in such abundance in our day was to work a thoroughgoing revival in the entire Church, this was necessarily going to have to include parishes. Since 98% or more of our people experience Church in parishes, I said, we were not going to be able to talk about the renewal of the whole Church unless something significant could happen in our parishes.

This, of course, was not terribly profound. But I went on to describe what a renewed parish might look like. The celebrations of the liturgy would be lively, with lots of participation. Our churches would be filled with enthusiastic worshippers, most of whom would get there early to get a good place to sit. The front rows would fill up first. The preaching would be powerful and combine with the rest of the celebration to bring people to conversion. We would begin to see, perhaps at first in a modest way, signs and wonders worked by the Lord to accompany the authentic proclamation of his word. Ministry visions would arise as the people touched by God's grace and brought along the path of personal renewal would begin to get prepared and sent out to do the Lord's work. There would be all kinds of ministries of evangelization, teaching ministries directed to people at various stages of spiritual growth, and ministries of caring that would reach out to the poor, the sick, the unemployed, the desperate, the lonely, the imprisoned, and scores of others who have been pushed to the margins of society. Relationships would be building and people would begin making commitments, not only to the Lord, but to one another as covenants would take shape. And last, but certainly not least, the pastors would concentrate on pastoring. Out of administration altogether, they would do what the apostles said they must do: get back *"to prayer and the service of the word"* (Acts 4:6).

The reaction was electric. I was amazed at the positive response the talk received. I was affirmed out of my mind. Of course, it was easy for me to talk. It is always easier to talk than to act. And, I guess, all present soon concluded it was nothing but a dream, a fantasy. But it was obviously what they were looking for, hoping, striving, and praying for.

All summer, as I prepared these presentations and dutifully gave them, I had a developing sense within me that the Lord had, as well, a personal word for me. It was as though he might have been telling me that the message I was delivering was from him alright and that I should give it as best I could, but, that when my summer run was finished, I should go home and stay quiet because he was going to change my agenda for me. I didn't know if I was hearing correctly (I fervently hoped I wasn't), but I just knew that, if my sense was correct, it surely meant parish for me, the thing I was talking so big about and had deliberately stayed away from for many years.

To shorten the story, the personal word turned out to be right on. I returned home late August, and, obedient to what I felt the Lord might be asking of me, I kept very quiet. Within weeks, I was appointed pastor of St. Mary's parish in Ottawa. It was, to say the least, an unlikely appointment. The clergy moves in our diocese are always made in June, not in September. However, there I was, after close to 30 years of ordination, a pastor for the first time.

St. Mary's is just on the edge of downtown, not really an innercity parish, but having some, at least, of the characteristics of one. It had been, 20 years and more previously, a busy, bustling parish, the church jammed to the doors several times each Sunday. There had been lots of involvement on the part of the parishioners. However, the years had taken their toll. Many of the people had moved away. The young families had seen the children into adulthood. The neighbourhood had undergone many changes. It just wasn't the same any more. The fall-away from the practice of the faith, evidenced across the whole, universal Church, was in clear focus here. Great numbers of people were simply staying away from church.

The congregation was now very small. My predecessor, a man I had known and respected for many years, using a suitably Canadian image, put it this way: "You can stand at the front of the church at any of the weekend Masses, and throw a snowball down to the back without hitting anybody." I thought he was kidding. He wasn't. The church was quite empty. He explained to me that there wasn't much going on. The only regular use of the parish facilities was a Brownie group that met Mondays at 4:30 in the afternoon. And they turned out to be a district group, not connected to the parish at all.

I panicked. I thought to myself: "I have made a horrible mistake taking this on. I wonder if I can possibly get out of it." I couldn't. I was stuck.

Although I was very distracted, not my usual calm self, there was one thing I had learned to do—get quiet every day for an extended time and pray. I consulted the Lord. I begged him for the wisdom to know what to do. I had to suppress my very natural tendency to try to get something going. Anything! In fact, I did try a couple of things that didn't work very well. I might have known and saved myself the trouble.

There are lots of good things we can do for God, thousands of things. The problem is that they will be our ideas, run on our energy and resources, won't work very well, and we'll exhaust ourselves in the process. How many highly motivated people have burned out trying to make good things happen for God?

What we need, I am convinced, is not a whole bunch of good ideas, but God's idea. He has a plan. If we can find out what it is and do it, it will work, work for him and for his kingdom.

So ... I persevered in prayer, seeking the Lord's particular word for the parish. Over time, I thought he might have been getting through to me. Having discerned correctly, I felt, the word about returning home after the summer and so on, I was developing a bit more confidence about my capacity to hear God speak. What I thought I was hearing this time, and it became clearer through a period of days and even weeks, was something like this: "I don't want you to do anything, except the very obvious things that a pastor must do. I want to take over here myself. I don't want any of your programs or ideas. I have a plan of my own. But, what I want from you is your permission. I want you to give me permission to do what I want to do. And, not only that, I want you to tell the people that you are giving me this permission, and that I want their permission, too. If I get enough permissions, I'll move. When I do, you'll see it. You can then point it out, and get everybody to support it."

Again, I was obedient to what I thought the Lord might be telling me to do. I gave him the permission he seemed to be asking for. In fact, I still give it to him — every day. Awkward though I felt about it, I did tell the people about it, Sunday after Sunday, and I did suggest to them that they might consider giving God the green light themselves.

Their reaction was, as I might have expected, interesting. It was easy to see they had never heard the Gospel call put quite that way. Of course, neither had I. I have heard it many times since from many different people, but, up to that point, early 1985, I had never heard it before. The people, I could tell, were struggling with it. I could see some of them mouthing the word 'permission' to themselves. The occasional one would turn to the person next, a spouse or whatever, and obviously ask: "What did he say?" The answer would come back just as obviously: "He said God wants your permission." Consternation all 'round.

I felt that the Lord was giving me different ways to say the same thing as, week in and week out, I tried the best I could to get the point across. I talked practically nothing else. "Let God be God," I would tell them. "He's good at it. God is very good at being God. Let's let him do what he wants here."

More shuffling in the pews. "Let's consult the Lord," I would say. "God has plans for our lives, both as individuals and as a body. If we consult him, maybe he'll tell us what they are." Furrowed brows. "Are we satisfied with the condition of the Church, with the condition of this parish?" I would rant on and on. "Are we satisfied with what's happened to our families, to the kids?" (Lots of tough things had happened of course: youngsters on drugs, gone from home, certainly gone from the Church, pre-marital arrangements, broken marriages, etc.) More were starting to listen. "Do we think God is satisfied? Do we think he has power to turn it around?" Some seemed to be getting interested. "Are we willing to let him change the things that we ourselves cannot change?" I could see some almost saying to themselves: "Is it really possible, I wonder?" "If we're willing to let God go to work," I would continue to belt it out, "then let's tell him so." "God is fed up being a spectator in our lives," I would belabour the point. "He wants to be a participant." This went on for over a year.

We were now involved in an extended waiting game, waiting for the Lord to move. To be very honest, I wasn't sure he would. We did have, however, what we thought was a word from him about the waiting. "I want you to become skilled," he seemed to be saying, "in **waiting** for me." A skill? It wasn't a gift then? He wouldn't help us to wait, it became clear. We had to decide to do it ourselves. As we made the daily decision and just plain waited, we would be leaving the door open for him to initiate the things he had in mind. If we were to get impatient and start a whole bunch of projects ourselves, we would just be cluttering up the path in such a way as to prevent him from moving freely. So, it was wait.

I'm not sure just exactly how long we did wait. There was no sudden breakthrough, I don't think. But, gradually, it began to dawn on me that the Lord was actually on the move.

People began at some point to testify to tears. Either they were crying in church themselves, or they saw somebody else crying. Oddly enough, it was mostly men who were doing the weeping. I thought at first they were just overwrought. They were losing their grip. Then I began to think: "Good heavens! Maybe they're crying because the homilies are so bad!" I finally realized what was happening one Sunday when a former student of mine, a chap who hadn't been to church in 11 years, since his final year of high school, came to Mass and, before the liturgy even started, broke down in tears that he couldn't control. He cried all through Mass. I met him afterwards. He was a mess. He said: "I don't know what's happening to me. I don't do this kind of thing. My life is in reasonably good shape, I think. I can't explain it." I wasted no time explaining it to him. God had touched his life. He has since been set on fire for the Lord and is one of our most involved lay ministers. He is busy now doing the Lord's work.

His story has been repeated again and again in the lives of many different people. But the action of God is both unmistakable and consistent. He is catching people's attention and turning them to him. People are getting converted right in the church in the middle of Mass.

What did it mean? What does it still mean? The Lord wants us, not only to notice what he's doing, but to understand what he's up to as well. He has placed, it seems evident, an anointing on the building itself and especially upon the celebrations that take place in it. He was telling us, we soon decided, that he wanted us to become very active in the work of conversion. He wanted us to become a parish placing a high priority on evangelization. We have become just that. We evangelize all over the place. All of our sacramental preparation ministries are evangelical in direction. Whether it be Baptism, First Confession, First Communion, Confirmation, or Matrimony, the teams' first aim is to evangelize those involved. We do street ministry. We go door to door. We run a coffee house downtown. "Are you folks really Catholics?" people will ask. "You bet we are," the answer will come back, "and we're proclaiming the same Gospel the Catholic Church has taught consistently for almost two thousand years."

When it first started to dawn on us that God was doing his favourite work in our midst, the work of conversion, we sent a few people away to get some training in how to evangelize. This is what we think the Lord meant when he said he wanted us to observe what he did, point it out and support it. When we saw what he was doing, we pulled the program in to support what he wanted done. This is a ministry principle of crucial importance. The priority is to find out what God is doing and go do it with him. If he has initiated it, it will have his power. We won't have to push it. We won't wear out trying to make it happen. The principle is simple once we see it in operation. He initiates. We support.

Conversions have continued unabated. People who have been away from the Lord and from the Church for years and years are coming back. First, they come to the Lord himself. At some point, he gets them to church. Some with no religious background whatever are hearing the Gospel for really the first time, responding to the Lord's call, and experiencing remarkable transformation as he goes to work within them.

But conversion has not been his only initiative. Ministry visions have been surfacing as the people the Lord is dealing with come alive in his grace and begin hearing his further call.

As I've already said, there are thousands of good things we can do for God. But, if we don't tune in to his plan and his timing, they'll have only limited effect. I have lots of ministry visions. But I have felt the Lord restraining me. I have felt he was saying one of his favourite words: "Wait!" My sense has been that he has wanted me to wait until a member of the congregation gets the vision and reports it to me. Then, and only then, should the ministry begin. So, that's what's happened. We have a good number of ministries. Many of them have come from the Lord through somebody in the pews. There are plenty more ministry visions, ones I'd love to see in place. But the time is not yet. We're waiting.

The most unexpected thing the Lord has done, as I see it anyway, is the development of a community of priests. Young men started gathering around who felt they were hearing a call to the priesthood. As we met together and persevered in seeking the Lord's word, he seemed to be giving us a vision for the community and its ministry. We were to come under the Lordship of Jesus with all that it implies, be devoted to the Eucharist, even to the establishing where possible of perpetual adoration, be open to using all the ministry gifts of the Holy Spirit, be consecrated to Jesus through Mary, be loyal to the pope and the Magisterium of the Church, live a simple lifestyle, and minister to the poor. It took hold and grew. A number of young men got on board. Now, priests are coming to join us. Never in my wildest nightmares did I ever see myself being involved in the establishment of a new community of priests. I always thought we had too many. Now I'm helping to organize another one. But, strange as it may seem, I'm convinced it's what the Lord wants.

The community, the Companions of the Cross, with a vision for ministry that all the members share, will be involved in the Lord's design for the renewal of the diocesan priesthood. They will pastor parishes and take on whatever other ministries bishops assign to them. In the parishes they pastor, when one moves out, another will move in, taking care, hopefully, of the problem that occurs too often when a pastor is re-assigned, having developed many good things, and a successor is named who takes over and cancels everything. We are not into cloning people, but we are quite determined to clone the vision.

Many good things have happened, instituted for the most part by the Lord himself. My impression is, however, that he has only begun. The parish is not a renewed community; it is merely in the process of being renewed. We have a long way to go.

But, that having been said, we have to admit it: interesting things are happening. Maybe we're not very different after all from the ordinary parish. Certainly, we are not unique. Interesting, I think, is the best word. The liturgies are joyful and seem to be life-giving. There are too many testimonies from people the Lord has reached for us to suggest they are not. The high Mass, in particular, is loud and long. Three hundred and more, close to half of the congregation, stay around for a good while after Mass to fellowship in the parish hall. The front rows fill up first. Many hands are held aloft in praise of God. We have even sung in the Spirit a few times. One person told me St. Mary's was the only church he'd ever been in where the people standing in the vestibule are singing. Conversions continue at a regular and encouraging pace. Many solid ministries have developed. In addition to the ones already mentioned, there are groups of young adults, high schoolers, young boys, young girls, children, a men's breakfast, a women's witness group, an outreach to the neighbourhood, and several others. Signs and wonders have begun to appear in a modest way portending greater things to come, I think. Relationships have been building and people are making commitments to one another. And … the pastors are pastoring and precious little else.

We do not sell charismatic renewal. We have a regular Monday night prayer meeting, but other than that we barely mention the word 'charismatic'. It is our firm conviction that the gifts of the Holy Spirit, including the peculiar charisms mentioned by St. Paul in his first letter to the Corinthians, are not meant to be the preserve of one particular movement in the Church, but rather are intended by God for the whole Church. Vatican II says so (Lumen Gentium 12). The present Holy Father, Pope John Paul II, says so as well (Christifideles Laici 20). When people call us a charismatic parish, as many do, my response is: "Not really. We are nothing more, nor less, than a **Catholic** parish in the fullest sense of the word."

Many people who visit us for the Sunday celebration will say something to us afterwards like: "How wonderful! How did you do it?" Of course, we have done none of it. We're just watching the Lord at work. We're not making it happen. We're letting it happen.

There is a question that very much needs an answer. Why is it that, although hundreds, even thousands, of our pastors have been very deeply touched by the Lord through this peculiar grace of the baptism in the Holy Spirit, there are not more parishes that are real beacons of renewal? Why is the landscape not fairly dotted with ports of call, places we could visit, places that are fairly bursting with the Lord's life, filled with enthusiastic believers?

I would suggest that there is an answer. There is a key to parish renewal. Our experience has taught us that the 'secret' is to give the Lord permission to work and to wait upon him. We are to
give him the green light, then to get out of the way and watch him go to work. How about: *"Leave it to the Lord and wait for him"* (Ps 37:7).

Does a pastor see renewal begin to take hold in his parish without taking any flack? Not at all. I have had nasty letters, ugly telephone calls, threats. I have been labelled a cult-master, a fanatic. I have been called insensitive. I have been shouted at on the church steps. I have been slandered. I have been accused of pandering to a right-wing group attracted by my conservative theology and preaching. I have been called a left-wing radical because of my emphasis on lay participation and lively liturgy. There have been walk-outs. Yes, there has been plenty of flack.

I believe the Lord wants us simply to stand in there and take it. It's all part of following Jesus. The Bible says: *"My son, if you come to serve the Lord, prepare yourself for trial"* (Sir 2:1). I know what it means.

When things started to happen and feathers started getting ruffled, I remember uneasily asking the Lord: "What if people leave?" I just felt he was replying: "Let 'em leave. For everyone that goes, I'll bring in ten more." That has just about literally been fulfilled. I have the impression God wants us to know that we have to fear only him.

It has to be made clear that the vision for the renewal of

the parish must come through the pastor. He's the one who has to call in the permissions for the Lord to inaugurate his plan. It won't do if the associate is the one with the vision. Or the prayer group. Or the housekeeper. Or the altar boys. It has to be the pastor. That's the way the Church works. That's the way the Lord has set it up.

The pastor has to set aside his fears about what may happen if he lets the Lord loose. He must put away his natural desire to please everybody and renew his commitment to please God alone. He will have to allow the Lord to unbusy his life, to cut him loose from the administrative trap in which so many of our pastors are caught. He must get used to standing around and watching for what God will do. He will have to give up his understandable desire to have a smoothly functioning parish and allow some of the chaos that goes on when God goes to work. And he must be willing to surrender his good reputation or what's left of it.

God wants to renew his Church. He has a carefully worked out plan. Let's allow him to get on with it.

Crisis in Masculinity

I spent 19 years of priesthood teaching high school. While I do not think, from my present perspective, that teaching is what the Lord has in mind for his priests, it certainly was a most enlightening experience for me. I liked it. I enjoyed it very much. I like adolescents a lot and related reasonably well to most of them. I don't know how much my students learned, but I learned plenty.

It was a small school, 300 or so, all boys for the first 12 years. All members of the staff had to be quite versatile, filling many different roles. One area in which I spent a good bit of time was Guidance. Many was the interview I had with young men. They would come to discuss their problems. Invariably the issue to begin with had to do with school. "I'm having trouble with my Geography," one would say, sounding me out. As he sensed he just might be able to talk to me, he would get around to what was really on his mind. Most often, the real trouble was at home. "I don't get along with my father," I would hear. "My father doesn't like me," another would say. "I can't talk to my father," was yet another common variation. It became like a broken record. It didn't take me too long to conclude that we had a major social problem on our hands, one that nobody seemed to be speaking or writing too much about.

Many of the boys had no fathers at all. Many more had fathers who, though living at home with them, were, for all practical purposes, emotionally absent. There were a number of very fine exceptions, of course. But, as I was beginning to see, the fatherson relationship was in big trouble.

The boys had many problems. Though some seemed relatively well balanced, an alarmingly large number were struggling with one thing or other. Some were nervous or insecure. Many were shy. Most had fears of one kind or other. Some were moody. A great many lacked confidence, self-esteem. Some struggled with loneliness or fairly deep feelings of inadequacy. There was much suppressed anger. There was a lot of sexual confusion. There were compulsive behaviour patterns. And many, many more.

In short, there was a whole baffling range of personality difficulties on my plate day after day, things that I found myself quite ill-prepared to handle. I'm not sure just how many of them I was able to help. My own understanding of human problems has, I think, come along only later in life.

But I have come to see the connection there is between the young man who struggles to make it emotionally in life and the boy who has an inadequate relationship with his father. Most of the problems the boys were trying to cope with were rooted firmly in their very manhood. They were basically not well fathered. They were part of what we could well call, particularly in our western society and culture, a growing social problem: a crisis in masculinity.

It isn't as though the fathers are especially to be blamed.

After all, who ever teaches men to be fathers? It seems to me that much more attention is given to preparing girls to be mothers. As a result, mothering is much better done. We can count our blessings in that regard. But we have to face up to the problem we do have. A lack of adequate fathering has produced for us several generations of unaffirmed men.

When I latterly taught girls as well as boys, I decided that they weren't, of course, fathered too well either. But for them, the issue didn't seem to be nearly as critical. In any case, the burden of this piece is the present condition of our men.

I think I understand the situation now in a way I didn't when I was teaching school. I'm not sure how well my theories would stand up to professional scrutiny, but I have developed a kind of homespun analysis.

As I see it, a boy's needs are met mainly by his mother for his first five or six years of life. However, at that point, which probably corresponds to the time when he will begin to spend full days at school, he should start to extricate himself gradually from the all-encompassing influence of his mother and commence to relate more immediately with his father. In the absence of a father, some effective substitute is critical—an uncle, an older brother, a teacher, or some other man who can give him quality time. He has to begin to understand in his quickly developing mind that he is a little man. He has to be able to say to himself, subconsciously: "I will be like him some day."

At this point in his life he needs more and more male attention. Between the ages of six and 12 or so, he will be entering into his identity as a man. He needs to spend time with his father, doing things, going places, sharing joys and struggles. He needs to be loved by his father. He needs to become accustomed to his father's arm around his shoulder. He needs to be respected for who he is and know that he is trusted. He needs to have realistic expectations laid upon him and be gradually given more and more freedom. And he needs his father to preside over this whole very important process.

To the degree that the process is successful, the boy will develop a sound emotional base, have a good sense of who he is, and be ready to enter into a more mature relationship with God.

If the process is not successful, he will become split off from one or more aspects of his masculinity. He may be deficient in his ability to concentrate, be lacking in ordinary courage, or have too little initiative. He may not be as dependable as he should be. He may become inconsistent. He may never be able to exercise authority properly. He may be indecisive. He may not be sufficiently assertive. He may experience sexual identity problems and be subject to homosexual inclinations. He may carry around a whole series of insecurities and fears. He will simply not be the man he knows he is supposed to be and that he desperately longs to be.

It has been said that the emotional package that each of us is today is the sum total of what we've been through. The experiences that have been most influential in shaping us are those of childhood. To the degree that our real needs have been met or not met we find ourselves as more or less adequate adult males. I suppose it is helpful for us to understand why we are the way we are. I believe God wants us to have such understanding. But there's more to it than that. Jesus came to proclaim good news, a fullness of life both here and forever. He means for his people to experience a fullness of joy as well, an abiding peace, and true freedom in him. He does not want us to be crippled by the emotional wounds we have received. There is healing for God's people. There is a way that he can get to the roots of our woundedness and set us free from the inadequacies that compromise our ability to function as his children the way he surely wants us to do.

The whole world of inner healing, the healing of memories, was a marvellous discovery for me. It was only after my high school teaching years that I became aware of it. Had I known then what I think I know now, I probably would have been able to help the young men far more than I did. I might have been able to lead some of them into the healing that they so obviously needed.

I would have known that God has the capacity to walk back into the past in our lives and supply the needs that were only inadequately met at the time so that we can experience the healing of present symptoms. In fact, God is present to all time in a way that we are unable to understand. For us, the past is gone. We can't go back. We can only remember. The future, for us, lies ahead. It is veiled from our eyes. For God, there is only the present. He can supply our past needs now. Among other things, he can father the unfathered.

Fairly recent neurological research has revealed that every single experience of our lives, beginning with our time in the womb, is registered in minute detail in our subconscious memories, including how we felt about them when they happened. Our subconscious is, they tell us, like a huge library of tapes. Perhaps we could say that God, in response to prayer, is able to remove enough of the unhealthy tapes and replace them with healthy ones, so that we can experience more and more freedom.

There is a crisis of masculinity in the world today. There are really very few men who are untouched by it in one way or other. The basic cause is a lack of adequate fathering. The good news is that God can turn it around.

CHAPTER TWO

Strategies for Today's Church

The Renewal of the Mind

St. Paul says: *"Do not conform yourselves to this age, but be transformed by the renewal of your mind so that you may judge what is God's will"* (Rom 12:2). He also speaks of bringing *"every thought into captivity and making it obedient to Christ"* (2 Cor 10:5). He likewise urges us to *"have the mind of Christ"* (1 Cor 2:16).

In order for my mind to be renewed, I must surrender it to the Lord. Many respond: "No way! That means giving up control of my life!" Precisely. Those are the Lord's terms. Total surrender. Being a disciple of Jesus in the full sense of the word, in the sense that he himself intends, means giving over to him my whole life. Including my mind.

Catherine Doherty, the Foundress of the Madonna House community in Combermere, used to tell her people that, if they wanted to be in tune with the Lord, they would have to "fold the wings of your intellect."

To most people, this all sounds fairly heavy. Does God want me to be a robot, some may ask? The answer, of course, is 'no'. He doesn't want to tamper with our freedom and won't. But he is truth itself, and wants us to embrace that reality in its fullness. To the degree that our minds are conformed to his, to that degree will we be free. Like him. But we have to choose him freely because we are human. That's the way we are—free. We are free like him.

A lot of people have difficulty surrendering to God. This seems particularly true in the case of those who are especially bright. I remember talking to one of my students a few years ago, an especially brilliant young chap. He was airing a number of the intellectual problems he was having with his faith. I suggested to him that his mind was getting in the way. I said something like: "God is bigger than your mind. It can never contain him. The Lord speaks, reveals himself, to the human heart. Even those with very limited intelligence can know God." He had never thought of it in that way and went off to ponder the whole thing some more.

The same thing came up in class another day. One of the young men, also quite bright, asked: "How is it that all geniuses are atheists? If the concept of God is so simple, why do they not grasp it?" It made for an interesting discussion. In the first place, not all geniuses are atheists. But, nonetheless, the world of academe is not generally noted for professions of faith. Why not? I would think it is simply that faith, a gift from God, is not an intellectual construct, and it comes from surrender to him, not from mental exercise. Those who have very high intelligence have a special problem to deal with in the matter of faith. The brighter a person is, the more he tends to assume that all truth is subject to human reason. But, the reality is that God transcends the human mind. Many academics seem to believe that there is nothing superior to the mind of man. Yet, God is just that.

More common is the position that God may well exist, and we should render him some obeisance, but he doesn't do anything or say anything, at least not any more. This stance has gained, I'm afraid, considerable headway among Christians. The one thing many people are not at all ready to hear is that it is possible to be in contact with the living God, to be in intimate relationship with him.

Jesus told us he would send us the Spirit of Truth, the promise of the Father. The Holy Spirit would, he said, lead us into all truth (John 16:13). When we make our surrender to the Lord, when we accept Jesus for who he is, and we ask him to give us his Spirit without reserve, we begin to know him, and the Father, and the Holy Spirit, in a whole new way.

It's called being baptized in the Holy Spirit. It is an enlightening of the mind, something that we allow and that God does. The Holy Spirit testifies in our spirits just who Jesus really is. It opens us up to receiving revelation from God. There develops in us a whole new awareness of the realm of the Spirit.

This is not a human achievement. It is not something that we can put together or figure out. Jesus put it this way: *"I praise you, Father, that you have hidden these things from the learned and the clever and have revealed them to the merest children"* (Matt 11:25).

To people who have become accustomed to dealing with God on an exclusively intellectual level, accustomed to relating to him as remote, the teaching on being baptised with the Spirit is a real confrontation. If we have become used to God's non-participation in our lives and in events around us, and if we have developed whole theological systems that accommodate themselves to that, the notion that God can break through into a lively relationship with us is bound to create some interesting discussion.

The spiritual awareness that takes over following our surrender to the Lord and our experience of the Holy Spirit, brings us face to face with another reality: the spiritual battle that rages around us. We begin to become painfully aware that there is an enemy who is bent on taking us captive.

"Our fight," St. Paul says, *"is not with mere flesh and blood. We contend with the principalities and powers, the rulers of this world of darkness, the evil spirits in the regions above"* (Eph 6:12). The world may think this is madness, but that's the way it is. Rather, it is madness to ignore it. We are the subject of the battle. The prize to the winner is the human mind. If Satan can capture our minds, or cloud them, or befuddle or benumb them, the rest is easy. The battle is not 'out there' somewhere. It's with me.

What are we to do? We must daily surrender to the Lord. We must guard the entrance to our minds. We must have some care as to what we allow in. What are we reading? What are we looking at? What are we talking about?

We must also listen carefully to the Church. The Lord speaks through the structures that he himself has set up. We can do no better than to have the mind of the Church.

It is important for us to stay sharp. It is important that we do not slip and get careless, that we do not become like the people St. Paul quotes Isaiah describing: *"The mind of this people has grown sluggish"* (Acts 28:27). We'll never be able to keep up with the Lord if we do. Surrendering to him is the key to the renewal of our minds.

Baptised with the Spirit

There are only four or five items that are recounted in all four Gospels. The synoptics—Matthew, Mark, and Luke—tell many of the same things, but John's work seems to be more of a supplement, filling in the gaps, recording events and teachings the other three don't mention. But one of the rare references that all four include goes something like this: *"There is one coming after me who is much greater than I, the strap of whose sandal I am not worthy to untie. I have baptized you with water, but he will baptise you with the Holy Spirit."* These words of John the Baptist, or words virtually identical, are found in Matt 3:11, Mark 1:8, Luke 3:16, and John 1:33. The connotation of being baptized has to do with 'being immersed in', or 'being plunged into', or 'being taken over by'. Jesus used the same expression in reference to the suffering he was to undergo (Mark 10:38-39). It appears the followers of Jesus were to be overtaken by the Holy Spirit.

In addition, Jesus himself makes reference to the same thing when, just before he ascended to the Father, he bids the disciples to wait in the city because *"within a few days you will baptized with the Holy Spirit"* (Acts 1:5).

The best definition of the experience of being baptized with the Spirit is to be found in a little book by Fr. Francis Martin. He says the expression is "a common way of describing a personal, abiding experience of the reality and presence of Jesus Christ, manifested in a transformed life and the use of spiritual gifts" (*Baptism in the Holy Spirit: A Scriptural Foundation*, p. 1).

We have to be careful not to confuse this reality with the sacraments of Baptism and Confirmation. We receive the Holy Spirit in Baptism when the Church gathers around us and celebrates this rite of Christian initiation. We are sealed with the Holy Spirit for ministry within the Church when we are confirmed. But the Church has always taught that, if the sacraments were received at ages too young for us to understand what was happening to us, we must, as we reach a time of sufficient maturity, affirm and make personal what was chosen for us in the actual sacramental encounters. When I freely choose to belong to Jesus, which is what my Baptism was all about, and ask the Lord to fill me with the Holy Spirit, which is what my Confirmation was all about, then his response to that will result in my experience of being baptized with the Spirit.

We must be careful, too, about the vocabulary we use to describe what we speak of here. It is incorrect, and quite misleading, to refer to this experience as 'the Baptism', or to recall it by saying: "I was 'baptized' one year ago today."

The experience of being baptized with the Spirit will certainly bring us into closer touch with the role of the Holy

Spirit in our lives and in the life of the Church than was ever the case before. We will know the Spirit of God as working in our lives. We will sense him doing the things Jesus taught that he would do. He will bear witness within me about who Jesus is (John 15:26). He will be teaching me things I hadn't effectively known before, in fact, all the things I need to know (John 14:26). We will begin to appreciate the particular actions of the Father, the Son, and the Holy Spirit. We will know the Father as the one who has the plans, whose will it is vital for us to do. We will know the Son, Jesus, as the one who links the human race to the Godhead, who makes it possible for us to enter into a share in the very life of God. We will know the Holy Spirit as the one who carries out the Father's directions, the one who gets things done, who has the wisdom and the power we need.

When I am baptized with the Holy Spirit, something happens to work a transformation within. My spirit is laid open to receiving revelation from God. I have an actual meeting with the risen Lord. I begin to know Jesus as alive. I develop a hunger to read and learn the written word of God. The Bible comes alive. I seem to receive a new pair of eyes to see what God is doing around me and a new set of ears to hear what he is saying. My priorities change. My conversation changes. I want to talk about the Lord.

A few years ago, a young man I knew, recently having experienced being touched by the Holy Spirit, went out for an evening to socialize with a group of his acquaintances. "How was it?" I asked him the next day. "It was very nice," he said. "It was great to see them all again. But there was something missing, and I'm not really sure what it was." "Did they talk about the Lord?" I asked. He realised then what had been missing. His old buddies were the same as always, actually quite a good bunch. But he himself had changed. What he really wanted to do was share stuff about the Lord.

The experience of being baptized with the Holy Spirit is, I'm convinced, supposed to be normative within the Church.

The Church is meant to be a body of people continually alive to God's presence, a people on fire for him. When we enter into the experience, we come to a new awareness of what the Baptist meant when he said: *"He will baptise you with the Holy Spirit and with fire"* (Luke 3:16).

Is it complicated to receive this touch from the Lord? Not at all. We have first to understand it, then to desire it, to repent of whatever sin there may be in our lives, to come freely under the Lordship of Jesus, and simply to ask the Lord to baptise us with his Holy Spirit. The rest is up to him, and he is very good at coming through.

Some years ago, when I asked the Lord to fill me with his Spirit, what followed was unmistakable. He changed me. I cannot say to others that I have something now that they do not have. But I can say that I have something now that I did not have. And it has made a world of difference in my life.

Gifts of the Holy Spirit

The positional statement of the Companions of the Cross states that we are to be open to using all the gifts of the Holy Spirit for ministry within the Church. There is to be no apologizing for these, no compromising. We are not to be manoeuvered into a position where the use of spiritual gifts has to be negotiated.

The Holy Spirit gives many gifts. The pages of the New Testament are crowded with testimony to that. But the gifts that we speak of here are those nine peculiar charisms that St. Paul writes about to the Corinthians. He speaks about the gifts of wisdom, knowledge, faith, healing, miracles, prophecy, distinguishing spirits, tongues, and interpretation of tongues (1 Cor 12:8-10).

We must take care to notice that Paul defines these precisely as gifts for ministry. They are not intended by God, then, for personal sanctification. They are to be used in the service of others. *"To each person,"* he says, *"the manifestation of the Spirit is given for the common good"* (1 Cor 12:7). They are not, it would seem, to be sought for their own sake, but to build up the Body of Christ. We must not become preoccupied with them. Neither should we set them aside as something we don't need.

A number of people contend that these particular gifts no longer exist in the Church and are not to be sought after at all. Their conviction is that they were only for the first ages of the Church, a special participation of the Holy Spirit intended to give the Lord's work an early shot in the arm to get it off to a good start.

It is surprising how many actually teach this. It is difficult to understand how they maintain such a position. The teaching of the Church is quite clear on the matter.

Vatican II explicitly states that the charisms under consideration here are for today's Church. Making specific reference to St. Paul's letter to the Corinthians, chapter 12, the Council Fathers declare: "Whether these charisms be very remarkable or more simple and widely diffused, they are to be received with thanksgiving and consolation since they are fitting and useful for the needs of the Church. Extraordinary gifts are not to be rashly desired, nor is it from them that the fruits of apostolic labours are to be presumptuously expected. Those who have charge over the Church should judge the genuineness and proper use of these gifts, through their office not indeed to extinguish the Spirit, but to test all things and to hold fast to what is good" (*Lumen Gentium* 12). That seems plain enough. The gifts are for today.

Pope John Paul II repeats at greater length what the Council has said. Here is some of what he says: "The Second Vatican Council speaks of the ministries and charisms as the gifts of the Holy Spirit which are given for the building up of the Body of Christ and for its mission of salvation in the world. Indeed, the Church is directed and guided by the Holy Spirit, who lavishes diverse hierarchical and charismatic gifts on all the baptized, calling them to be, each in an individual way, active and co-responsible" (*Christifideles Laici 21*). Again, very clear.

These charisms ordinarily become activated in people's lives when they experience what is known as being baptized with the Spirit. This is a spiritual awakening that occurs in the life of the believer who repents of whatever sin may exist in his life, freely places his whole being under the Lordship of Jesus, and simply asks the Lord to baptise him with the Holy Spirit. Some prefer to call it an outpouring of the Spirit. Yet others speak of an infilling of the Spirit. Whatever we call it, it's real, and it is most often accompanied by an ongoing manifestation of these peculiar charisms of the Holy Spirit.

One possible explanation of each of the nine charisms is in order.

1. **Wisdom.** Our faith tells us that God has specific plans for his people—for the whole Church, for smaller bodies of believers, and for the individual as well. The word that gives us his direction is known as wisdom. It is, then, his 'now' word for us. When we think we are hearing it from him, we have to discern it properly and test it out. Though we can often get it wrong, it is well worth pursuing on a regular basis.

2. **Knowledge.** If we are ministering to someone or a group of people, and we seem to have come to some kind of impasse, the Lord may give us an inner word, some kind of enlightenment to assist us to do his work. This would be a piece of information that we ordinarily could not get hold of. This should be familiar to the Church. St. John Vianney ministered with this gift continually. He would know people's sins before they confessed them. It is not reading minds. It is a gift of knowledge. Like wisdom, this, too, must be discerned and tested out.

3. **Faith.** This is not the same as the ordinary gift of faith which the Lord gives us when we surrender to him, that assurance that what we believe is true. This is an extraordinary gift of faith which will tell us what God is going to

do. St. Luke gives us the example we need. He recounts that, when Paul was preaching in Lystra, there was, in the group of listeners, a man who was lame from birth. He says: *"Paul looked directly at him and saw that he had the faith to be cured"* (Acts 14:9). Paul then told the chap to get up and walk, and he was healed in an instant. The gift of this particular kind of faith operated in both of them. God disposed the man to receive the healing and revealed to Paul that he, the Lord, would cure him if Paul would call it out. Jesus healed in the same way. He did only, he tells us, what he saw the Father doing (John 5:19). He knew what his Father was going to do. That's the gift of faith we refer to here.

4. **Healing.** This is one we are familiar with, if not, perhaps, from personal experience, certainly from reading, not only the Scriptures, but the chronicles of the Church. There have been many strong healing ministries. Brother André of Mount Royal is one most Canadians have heard of. It is important to note that it is not the minister of healing who receives the gift, but rather the person who gets healed. He is the one who receives the gift. The one who prays for him simply ministers it.

5. **Miracles.** These are occurrences which go beyond the laws of nature. When Jesus walked upon the water, this was a miracle. When he fed the multitudes, this, likewise, was a miracle. Those who are familiar with the ministry in El Paso of Fr. Rick Thomas and his team will know that the miracle of the multiplication of food still happens in our day.

6. **Prophecy.** A prophet is one who speaks for God. A word of prophecy, if it is authentic (and it must be discerned), conveys some message to us from the Lord. A prophetic utterance is often spoken in the first person, after the manner of the Old Testament prophets, as though God

himself is doing the talking and choosing the words. It doesn't have to be that way. If we feel we might have some sense of what God wants to say in a particular situation, we can simply say so. It isn't necessary to phrase it in first person style. Most of the 'prophecies' I have heard at meetings, though very nice, were not, I feel, actual words from God. A lot of them were nice, comforting thoughts, but possibly proceeded more from the person speaking them than from God.

7. **Distinguishing Spirits.** The reality of the spiritual battle that goes on around us is something most of us would rather not know too much about. Yet, it's going on. And it can have profound effect upon us. Evil spirits can influence people and events. This gift enables us to tell when something is coming from God and when it, perhaps, has some other source.

8. **Tongues.** The gift referred to here is one which has place at a meeting, an assembly or liturgy at which we are rendering worship to God. A person will speak out in an unfamiliar language (or language-like sounds). This has an arresting effect on those present. When it is authentic, it is the Lord's way of catching our attention so that we will listen carefully to what follows. St. Paul gives an extensive teaching on this in his first letter to the Corinthians, chapter 14. The people there were making entirely too much use of this gift, and he writes to call them back into the Lord's order. There are other gifts of tongues, one of which is a ministry instrument as well. This comes into play during prayer ministry when the one praying is not sure what to pray for. St. Paul addresses this in his letter to the Romans when he says: *"The Spirit, too, helps us in our weakness, for, when we do not know how to pray as we ought, he will himself make intercession for us with groanings that cannot be expressed in speech"* (Rom 8:26). There is an additional gift of tongues, used in giving praise to

God. But this is more for personal edification than for ministry.

9. **Interpretation of Tongues.** When tongues have been used to speak out at a public gathering, the attention of those present having been caught, something is now required in the vernacular so that everybody will have an idea of what the Lord has in mind. If the original intervention has been authentic, there will follow an 'interpretation' in the language of the place. When it is authentic, it ends by being a prophetic word upon which the Lord seems to want to lay particular emphasis.

Not all of these charisms have been common through the history of the Church. Some have been in more frequent use than others. The same can be said for our own day. But, nonetheless, when genuine, they are all from God himself. They all have their own proper use. They are meant for ministry within the Church. Do we need them? We need all the help we can get.

It is said that St. Thérèse of Lisieux experienced one day in prayer an unusual vision. Many of the gifts of the Holy Spirit were laid out before her, as it were, on display. She heard the Lord inviting her to choose one. Her response was: "I'll take them all, if I may." She had the right idea.

Wisdom

There are many biblical references to wisdom. The one I have found most arresting is Proverbs 4:7. The inspired writer says: *"The beginning of wisdom is: get wisdom! At the cost of all you have, get understanding."* The effect of that line has been, not only to convict me that wisdom is important, but to set me upon a quest to discover its full implications.

The letter of St. James is reassuring. The author advises us: "If you want wisdom, ask for it" (Jas 1:4). It would appear then, that, whatever wisdom is, the Lord is willing to give it to us.

The text that begins, however, to uncover for me the full

meaning of wisdom is from St. Paul's letter to the Colossians. He says: *"I have been praying for you that you might have full knowledge of God's will through perfect wisdom and spiritual insight"* (Col 1:9).

So that's it, then. Wisdom is God's particular word for me? I think so. In the light of this, other Scriptures begin to fall into place. The Church in Antioch received the Lord's word of wisdom when, as St. Luke writes it, *"they were one day engaged in the liturgy of the Lord. The Holy Spirit spoke to them, saying: 'I want Saul and Barnabas set aside for the work I have in mind for them'"* (Acts 13:2). A word of wisdom! Delivered, no doubt, in prophetic style and confirmed by all present.

Paul's ministry would continue in this way. In Acts 16, he and his team are making their way through Asia Minor. On two occasions, they were inclined to head in directions that made sense to them on a purely human level, but the Holy Spirit re-directed them. God, it would seem, had another idea. Eventually, his word was conveyed to them in a prophetic dream that Paul himself experienced. Wisdom again.

Jesus himself, operating fully in the spiritual gifts, puts it in an interesting way. He says: *"The Son does only what he sees the Father doing"* (John 5:19). He does only what his Father indicates to him. He does his Father's will. In fact, he tells us: *"My food is to do the will of the one who sent me"* (John 4:34).

Can we conclude, too, that the Lord's plan for us, in our day, is the same as it was in the early Church? Why not? We were never given any indication that things would change. In fact, Jesus said he would be with us to the end of time (Matt 28:20). He said that we would do the same things as he himself was doing (John 14:12).

If the Lord has plans for us, it would seem to go without saying that it is important for us to find out what they are. I, for one, certainly want to know what he's got in mind. As I see it, the beauty of God's will is that, when we carry it out, it works. It gets the job done. My own personal conclusion is that it's the only thing worth doing. Nothing else in the whole world is worth doing more than the will of God.

There is such a thing as human wisdom. Someone with a certain shrewdness is said to be a wise person. One who makes effective decisions, one who has "the smarts", is much admired and envied. But all the wisdom on earth does not compare to divine wisdom, the gift of God, insight into his very will for me and for us. That's the wisdom I want.

If the Lord has a plan for us, we have to assume first, that he is willing to convey this wisdom to us, and second, that there is a way we can get hold of it.

There is often much frustration here. I have heard so many people say that, no matter how hard they have tried to find out God's will, he just never comes through for them. I think they are probably exaggerating, but it may simply be, too, that they just do not know how to go about it. I would suggest seven practical steps.

1. The teaching on wisdom has to be understood and believed. It has been my conclusion for some time that most people in the Church simply do not know that the Lord has fairly specific plans for them and that they can find out what they are. We have to believe that God is anxious to communicate with us, and would do just that, if only we would get serious about hearing from him.

   One Christian leader that I have listened to says he's convinced that God is bombarding the Church with information, but that most of it is falling on deaf ears. We are just not listening. And we're not listening because we actually don't believe, in any effective way, that all of this is true.

2. We have to want to do the Lord's will. We have to be people who mean it when we pray: Thy will be done on earth as it is in heaven. We have to realize how attached we are to doing our own will and begin pulling away from that. We have to have a real desire to do what God wants.

3. If we want to know the Lord's will, if we want the wisdom, we have got to ask (Jas 1:4). A priest I know and admire says that he and his parish core group of intercessors and ministers were gathered in prayer a few years ago seeking the Lord's direction for the parish. They felt they needed his wisdom, but weren't entirely sure what that meant. They persevered in prayer, asking God what wisdom was. One evening, as they met together, they received in prophetic mode a word they truly believed was God's answer to their question. It went something like this: "You ask me what wisdom is. A good question. Listen, and I will tell you what it is. Ask me everything! That's wisdom."

   So there it is. The Lord wants to tune us in to his plan. But we have got to ask. It is unlikely that he would be able to do much instructing on behalf of a people who were not asking.

4. We have to seek the Lord's will while telling him that we will do it whatever it is. If any of these steps is the key, this is the one. Before we even know what it is, we are telling God that, once he conveys his plan to us, it's as good as done. His wish is our command. It's not as though we'll think about it once he tells us. He's got our 'yes' before he speaks.

   There is nothing new about this. It's called abandonment to the will of God. The pages of Church history are crammed with the writings of saints and other spiritual giants who have called for this again and again.

   Some people find this a rather daunting step to take. One young man of my acquaintance, having undergone a powerful conversion, a very dramatic touch from the Lord, was pledging to me how he was now going to follow the Lord with all his heart. I asked him if he was willing to tell God he would do his will no matter what, even before knowing it. He at first said: "Of course." But he seemed to change his mind quickly when he added: "But what if he wants me to be a priest? Anything but that!"

Until we say the prayer of abandonment, the Lord will have difficulty getting through to us. He wants our offer with no strings attached. Until he gets it, we'll be spending a lot of time wondering what he's saying to us.

5. The will of God, his 'now' word for us, his wisdom, can come to us best in the context of committed relationships. I cannot assume with confidence that I have heard the Lord correctly until it is discerned for me by those to whom I have committed myself.

    I am always very uncomfortable when someone tells me that he or she is sure the Lord has spoken. "Has it been discerned with your committed brothers and/or sisters?" I will ask. "No," will be the reply, "but I am sure just the same." With all due respect to many prayerful people I have met, I'm afraid this doesn't work well at all.

    Some object that this cannot work for them because they have no real, effective, committed relationships in their lives. I would have to make the point that, nonetheless, this is God's plan for us. Community is not an option. It can take many different forms, but community is not an option. My strong suggestion is that, in the absence of committed brothers or sisters, we pray very sincerely to the Lord to lead us to the people with whom he wants us to share our lives. I don't know of any instance where there has been serious prayer about this that the Lord hasn't come through.

6. Once we have got this far, we have now to wait upon the Lord. If being abandoned to God's will is the key, waiting is the toughest part of the whole equation.

    Very shortly after we felt we had a clear word from God that he wanted a new community of priests, one that would later be called the Companions of the Cross, we felt he was giving us some strong advice. "I want you," he seemed to be saying, "to become skilled at waiting for me."

We found this an intriguing notion. Not only was waiting important, it was a skill. It was not a gift. We could not ask the Lord to give it to us. We had to decide to do it. It was like trusting in God. It was like getting up in the morning. It was like forgiveness, and it was like love. All are basic decisions which, when made and persevered in, become skills.

People ask if, while waiting, they are simply to do nothing. The answer to that is no. God doesn't want us to sit in a corner watching the world go by. We are to move ahead doing the things the Lord has already told us to do, the things that pertain to our states in life, and the things that are just obvious. (I am coming more and more to believe that the Lord is very enthusiastic about our use of the common sense he has given us.) As we move ahead with these, he will catch up with us along the way with the word he wants us to have. Psalm 37:7 puts it this way: *"Leave it to the Lord and wait for him."*

7. When we have run a potential word through the previous six steps and feel it may qualify as authentic, we have now to act on it, to test it out. If God blesses it, we will conclude we have got hold of a genuine direction from him. Through this, we will become more and more familiar with how God wants to speak to us and have more and more confidence in our capacity to hear him with some accuracy.

Those are the seven steps. They are not designed to command a word from God or to box him in. Rather, they are intended as a help to us as we try to hear what he is saying to us.

God's word can come to us in many ways—as we read Scripture, as we share with brothers and sisters, as we spend time in quiet prayer, as we pray together with a group, through coincidences or unexpected happenings, and many others—but, as we become practised in catching the Lord's direction, we will come to the point at which we, as often as not, will recognize an authentic word when we hear it. There will be a response in our spirits and a peace in our hearts that will be hard to mistake.

A final word of caution is needed here. We must not take ourselves too seriously. We have to know that it is alright with God if we get it wrong. We have to know that he can deal with our mistakes, that his plan is very flexible, that he can mend the honest damage we might do. Honest mistakes are part of the learning process. The Lord deals with us as we are: imperfect and fallible human beings. While we must take the Lord very seriously, we must not do the same with ourselves.

The wisdom of God is one of the basic assumptions upon which the spirituality of the Companions of the Cross is built. We relentlessly pursue the Lord's word. We make no major moves without it. We've made mistakes, but we have to admit it: we've got it right a few times, too.

Ministry

Every member of the Church is called to ministry in the Lord's name. This call derives from each one's Baptism. Vatican II makes this abundantly clear. Although all must be done in order and every ministry must be exercised in submission to some lawfully established authority within the Church, the call is from the Lord himself and the pastors of the Church must search out those whom God is gifting and confirm his call.

I didn't always see it this way. In fact, my seminary training prepared me for a very different model of ministry. In accepting the Lord's invitation to the priesthood, I understood that I was becoming a member of that dauntless band of men upon whose shoulders rested the sometimes burdensome task of 'running' the Church. Priests were what the Church was all about.

Our first priority, it seemed to us, was to make the Mass and the Sacraments as available as possible. This led us to multiply Masses, often cramming as many as we could into the permitted hours. (No celebration of the Eucharist was allowed after 1 pm.) A parish I helped out at in the late fifties and early sixties had Sunday Masses at 7, 8, 9, 10, 11, 12, and 1. This necessitated neat, efficient liturgies, correct but somewhat rushed, the clearing of the parking lot between Masses being of prime importance. I must confess this was a particular sore point with me (I'd had a bit of exposure to the liturgical movement), but there was really nothing I could do about it.

In addition, long hours were scheduled for Confessions in most parishes and penitents were shuffled through at a fairly rapid clip. There wasn't very much time to give much individual attention to those who might have needed it.

Baptism was administered without much preparation, and the other Sacraments suffered varying degrees of the same fate.

But the important thing was to make the Sacraments available. It was as though they were able to work automatically, and, as long as people received them often enough, all would be well. Ex opere operato was pretty well our working principle. If people wanted to grow in their faith, they were advised simply to receive the Sacraments more often. If they were alienated from the Church, they were said to be 'away from the Sacraments', and the solution for them was to 'get back to church'. If they would only do this, their chances for salvation were once again deemed to be promising.

Of course, making the Sacraments available was something only a priest could do. The ministry of the Church was seen as flowing exclusively from the ordained clergy. The rest of our time was taken up instructing potential converts to the Church, visiting parish schools, organizing and attending meetings, listening to people's troubles, and taking care of the material administration of the parish plant. The last-named was considered to be the preserve of the pastor alone and tended to consume a large portion of his time.

There was very little room in all of this for lay people to exercise their own apostolate. It was assumed that all gifts for ministry resided in the priesthood. The solution for any problem of deficiency in ministry was more priests. Our inability to answer completely the needs people had for ministry was blamed on the perennial 'shortage of priests'. Just how short we were of clergy is open to debate. One of our parishes had a staff of four priests appointed full-time. And religious communities were able to do better still. One of the 'order' parishes in town regularly had six or seven priests on the roster with one or two religious brothers as well!

The lay person's participation in parish ministry was pretty well limited to very temporal matters. The 'spiritual' mission of the parish was left almost entirely to the clergy and the religious.

Vatican II has restored to the Church a more balanced and authentic model of ministry. We must note that it is something 'restored'. It is not new. Not only is it reflected in Scripture, it finds its place in the Church's own history and experience. The priest becomes, not the only minister within the parish, the principal minister among many. His is the task to co-ordinate the ministries.

He must make his own the vision and mission of the whole, universal Church. He must take on the whole burden of Jesus himself—the extension of the kingdom of God to every human being. No longer can his concern only be to keep the parish going. Jesus founded the Church so that all could be redeemed and brought into God's family.

The scope of the work is enormous. The Church is commissioned to reach out and bring the Good News to everyone: nonbelievers as well as believers, unchurched as well as churched, the wounded and the healthy, people of all ages, backgrounds, and occupations. The mandate is to evangelize everyone fully and bring each into a personal relationship with the Lord. The assignment is to speak a prophetic word of justice and peace to a broken world and to work toward achieving it. And the call includes the celebration of the Lord's mighty deeds in regular, joyful, meaningful liturgy. For the Church's mission to be successful, all this has to be happening in every parish.

The priest has to realize that, although he bears the ultimate responsibility, he does not have to do it all.

The Council has made it plain that all the gifts needed for ministering to the Church and to the world are present in the Body of Christ. It is the pastor's role to identify the gifts and call them forth. He must see to the training of those called and send them out. He must then continue to work with them and support them.

Since most of these lay people will have only a limited amount of time to give to ministry, there will have to be a great many of them. Although their apostolate derives, as the Council makes clear, from their Baptism, it must, to be in the order the Lord intends, be exercised in submission to the pastor. Just as the priest's ministry is out of order unless it is in union with that of the bishop, so the lay person's ministry makes no sense unless it is done in concert with and directed by the pastor.

All of this presupposes that a pastor exercise his ministry as the head of a team. There is no way he can do it alone. There is no way the Church can be properly present to the world in all its needs without fully putting to use all the gifts the Lord is willing to give his people. It is not enough for them to be urged from time to time to 'get out there and do it'. There needs to be recognition that not every person's gifts are the same and that giftedness without training will be largely ineffective.

In short, it remains the pastor's task to head a sizeable team of people in his parish to make it possible for the Church's mission to be adequately carried out.

The reality we face, and the principal problem, as I see it, is that we priests have little training to do the kind of pastoring that Vatican II calls us to do. We need to be co-ordinators of ministries, and we are ill-equipped to do the job.

One of the frustrations that I experience regularly is running into eager lay people who, though obviously gifted to minister, have little opportunity to get involved in the Church's mission. I would venture to say that the pews in virtually all of our churches are fairly bulging with gifted people who are both capable of significant contribution to the real work of the Church, very enthused about it, and ready to give of their time, money, and effort to get it done.

It is time for lay people to come back into their own. It is time for the pastors of the Church to call them into it.

Evangelization

Evangelization has been, from the beginning, the Church's principal mandate. It "exists," in fact, as Pope Paul VI has said, "to evangelize" (*Evangelii Nuntiandi* 14). Jesus left the Church to do his work, to bring the good news of life to the ends of the earth. All people are to know that God, their Father, loves them and has an intense desire to share his own very life with them both now and forever. The process of conveying that good news is called evangelization.

Authentic evangelization aims at bringing the individual person into a personal relationship with the Lord God himself, with Jesus, and with the Holy Spirit. The old catechisms well summed up mankind's basic purpose—to know, to love, to serve God in this world and to be happy with him forever in the next. Evangelization is concerned with the first step— knowing God. The Lord is knowable. Just as we can know one another, we likewise can know the Lord. He lives. He can reveal himself to us and will, if we let him. This is the work of evangelization—opening people up to a real contact with the living God.

Evangelization works a great change in people. Through it the Lord transforms lives. People, once evangelized, are often never the same again.

Those who are effectively evangelized begin to manifest some common characteristics. They become enthused about their faith and living it out. Their patterns of conversation change. They begin to want to talk about the Lord and what they think they see him doing and hear him saying. Their involvement in the liturgy and ministries of the Church becomes of prime interest. They develop a hunger for learning the Scriptures. No longer are these meaningless. And they become eager, even sometimes to the point of making pests of themselves, to share with others what they believe they have received from the Lord.

Evangelized people are different. They often become the backbone of the Church and their pastors find themselves running to catch up.

What is it, really, that changes them? How does it work?

The evangelization dynamic is really very simple, but probably not very well understood. The Magisterium understands it. This is evident from official statements and decrees. But the rank and file of the Church does not seem to be clear about it at all.

Evangelization, as I have observed it, is a three-step process.

1. The presentation of the Gospel challenge. Basically, Jesus invites us to follow him, to surrender all to him, to make him Lord of our lives. That comes first.

2. The hearers respond, hopefully in the affirmative. They decide to accept the invitation. They claim the Lordship of Jesus over their lives.

3. God acts. He stirs up the Holy Spirit in the souls of the baptized (or gives the Spirit to the unbaptized), and they begin to undergo a significant transformation in their lives.

How does it happen? God makes it happen. It is the third step of the process that makes the difference. And it is this third step that most people in the Church simply do not understand. It cuts across the commonly held assumption that Jesus has left the Church on its own, that he was only kidding when he said he would always be with us. And it contradicts the prevailing assumption that God is remote, that he perhaps is disinclined to get involved in the lives of his people, that he is content to be a spectator in our lives rather than a participant.

Properly understood, evangelization is something that we start and that God finishes. The proclamation is human. The response is human. But, what follows is divine. God intervenes. Through effective evangelization, we are opening the door for God to get intimately involved in the lives of his beloved sons and daughters, something that he is most anxious to do.

Only God can change a human heart. Try as we might, we can only prepare the way.

Evangelization, however, does not stand alone. Although it comes **first,** it is **not** the Church's only ministry. Evangelization does not make people perfect. Without the other ministries of the Church, with evangelization alone, we will have just a group of people all dressed up with nowhere to go.

Evangelization does not bring instant wisdom or prudence. The evangelized can often be like bulls in a china shop. They can be elitist. They can degenerate into a 'me and God' spiritual life. They can become focussed upon experiences of the Lord instead of upon the Lord of the experiences. Misdirected enthusiasm can produce a lot of chaos.

Evangelization is not enough. Once evangelized, people need to be catechized, discipled, pastored, and prepared for ministry within the Church. Evangelization is not enough. But it is the pre-requisite for everything else. Unless we evangelize properly, the other things we try to do just won't work very well.

Has the Catholic school system over the years catechized well? I think so. The catechetical movement has made great strides. We have learned how to talk about the Lord. We know how to teach people about him. We have found more and more effective ways to convey information about God.

Has the Catholic school system by and large produced young men and women who are enthused about their faith, anxious to be involved in the liturgy and ministries of the Church, keen to share with others what the Lord has done for them, hungry for the word of God? We know it hasn't. Why not? Very simple. We have not evangelized. We have given people lots of information about God, but we haven't led them to him. Many wind up knowing about God, but not knowing him.

Father Robert Wild of Madonna House in Combermere understands it well, I believe. He claims that we have to question our capacity to teach anybody anything at all about the faith until the person is first, at least to some significant degree, evangelized. This is how he puts it: "This is basically what the Spirit has taught us in the charismatic renewal—the tremendous importance of such an experiential encounter with God. We have discovered that, without this, most of our catechesis is backwards. Trying to give 'religious instructions' to people who have not experienced God the Father through the Spirit of Jesus is not only enormously difficult, but one wonders if it should be done at all" (*The Post-Charismatic Experience*, p. 25).

Evangelization's purpose is conversion. Evangelization is a ministry. Conversion is a grace. Evangelization is our work, given to us by the Lord. Conversion is his work. When evangelization is done properly, he releases his grace. People get converted. Their attention is caught. They are, like St. Paul, captured by their Saviour (Phil 3:12). They reassess all other things in the light of their knowledge of him (Phil 3:8).

The evangelization/conversion dynamic is a process. It may take place quickly or over a period of time. The Lord is very respectful of his people. Some, because of the circumstances of their lives, need time. We do not teach evangelization/conversion as instantaneous. It can happen that way. God can do anything. But, perhaps, more often, it takes a while. The ones who minister evangelization, the evangelists, need to have a sensitivity born of the Spirit. They must not be the types that 'blow in, blow up, and blow out.' They must meet people where they are.

They must stick around. They must walk along with people.

Evangelization proclaims Jesus. It does not apologize for him. He, after all, said of himself: *"I am the way, the truth, and the life; No one comes to the Father except through me"* (John 14:6).

It is difficult to understand how some within the Church are now telling us that we must not try to convert people, must not intrude upon their space, must respect where they are. It is as though they are suggesting to us that there are many roads to the Father. In fact, there is only one—Jesus, his Son. He is to be proclaimed.

It is likewise difficult to understand why some are suggesting to us that other ministries of the Church are to come before evangelization. We hear that the social gospel must take precedence. That people cannot hear the Gospel until they are fed, clothed, housed, and employed. The Church's social teachings are indeed clear. And to be authentic witnesses to the Gospel we must be serving people's obvious needs. But these ministries must follow evangelization, not go before it. Jesus himself said the cup of water was to be given in his name (Mark 9:41). Unless we be evangelizers, we will simply be social workers, development workers, health care workers, and educators. Noble works all, but without evangelization, they can be merely human effort. Unless we evangelize, we can be involved in purely human work. We can try to do good things for God, but unless we are doing them God's way, at his direction and in his time, we will be running only on our own strength and resources. This is a recipe for frustration and burn-out.

Archbishop Plourde has told the Companions of the Cross

that he wants us to be, above all, an evangelizing body. In all we do, we are to carry with us the Gospel of Jesus, the fullness of life.

Thus, the Church's number-one priority has become the same for the Companions of the Cross. We will evangelize first, last, and always. We will serve the poor, alienated Catholics, youth, and any others that our bishops direct us to serve, but we will try to evangelize them as we serve. We will try in every way possible to help the Catholic Church to recover an effective ministry of evangelization and to become once again what it once essentially was—an evangelical Church. The Catholic Church, the Church that Jesus founded, the Church of the ages, must once again lead the way.

Jesus has bidden his Church first and foremost to bring the Gospel to all mankind, to evangelize with all their hearts. The Companions of the Cross pledge themselves to that.

Ministry Hazards

Reading, not so long ago, through a little book by the late Don Basham, called *True and False Prophets*, I came to a deepened awareness of a somewhat frightening truth: good ministry can come through an unworthy minister. It isn't that I hadn't known that before, but the examples he gave and the way he put it drove the point home in a way that I hadn't experienced before.

Here are a few of his statements: "A pure word can come through a perverted mouthpiece," and, "A powerful ministry entitles a man to no special protection from God," and, "Dazzled by signs and wonders, we can fail to exercise proper discernment about a particular ministry or the person himself," and, "Successful ministry is not an indication of probity of life." I find that pretty disturbing stuff.

He included several examples of what he meant. Without, of course, revealing any identities, he showed how great things have happened, great things for God, through people whose lives were grossly out of order.

How easily we can be deceived! Do we not tend to think of success in the things we do as signs of God's favour? Mother Teresa's word is surely apropos. "The Lord does not call us to be successful," she says. "He calls us to be faithful."

We must protect one another. We are called to be ministers of the Lord's word and healing. We are subject to all the hazards of such ministry. Our work for the Lord can be very up-front, very much in the public eye. If something good happens through us, many people will assume it has something to do with us. And they'll be sure to tell us so. And, human as we are, we are liable to start believing it. We can begin to think of the ministry as 'ours'. It can become important for us to be successful.

How good of the Lord to let us fail at times, to let us fall on our faces and look bad. What a protection for us! In a very real way, we have to beware of success.

We have to be accountable. A community can be a great protection, brothers who can keep us on our toes and prevent us from getting swelled heads.

It is better if we, where it is possible, minister together with someone else or with a whole team. Lone rangers will inevitably run into trouble.

It is important that we never minister at all without a proper mandate, without being sent out by the authority to which we are subject. *"Self-styled apostles"* (Rev 2:2) have always been the bane of the Church, even from the earliest times.

Successful ministries have an unfortunate tendency to begin competing with one another. There is an actual spirit of competition that we must be aware of and rebuke regularly. We must guard against contending with one another or with any ministries within the Church anywhere. Our competition is not with one another. It is, as St. Paul emphasizes, with the *"principalities and powers"* (Eph 6:12).

Several years ago, with thoughts of this kind in my head, I piously asked the Lord to make me invisible, to get the work done in such a way as to reflect all the credit upon himself, and in a way that nobody would notice me. Shortly after that, I gave a talk at some gathering, an address that I worked very hard at preparing and that went, I thought, extremely well. People seemed very attentive while I was speaking. When the meeting broke up and everybody was mingling, socializing, and fellowshipping, not a word was spoken to me about how well I had done. Driving away in my car a little later, I found myself thinking: "How do you like that! No affirmation for the talk at all. What's the matter with those people?" Very quickly, I thought I heard the Lord speaking in my heart: "But I am simply answering your prayer. I am making you invisible." I wasn't sure how much I enjoyed being invisible, but I had certainly received a direct answer to my request.

Perhaps it would be best if we told the Lord that our desire is that all the significant ministry, all the use of powerful gifts, be exercised by someone else. As long as the Lord's work gets done, what difference does it make who does it?

We need to be protected from the hazards that are built into the ministry we undertake. Let's keep it in mind and protect one another.

CHAPTER THREE

Growing into Discipleship

Just as Jesus called those who would listen to leave all things and follow him, so today the Lord calls as many as will hear him to make everything in their lives over to him and to make themselves fully available to him for his purposes here on earth.

Salvation is offered to us as a free gift. Jesus has paid the full price for our entry into eternal life. We have been purchased by his saving death on the Cross. But salvation is not discipleship. Those who want to follow the Lord's call to give their lives over to him completely need to know that the cost of this discipleship is total. He wants everything.

It is a wonderful call. The cost may be high, but the dividends are terrific. Not only in heaven, but right here right now. Those (whether married or single) who may be hearing the Lord's call into total commitment to him would do well to consider it carefully. For my own part, I consider the decision to go all-out for God to be the smartest move I've ever made.

Repentance

The goal of the disciple of Jesus is to be conformed fully to the Father's will, to approach more and more closely to the kingdom of God. Jesus always did the will of the Father. He said: *"My food is to do the will of the one who sent me"* (John 4:34). The fullness of the kingdom was present in him. Though tempted like us, Jesus, the very Son of God, was not bogged down by sin the way we are (Heb 4:15). For us, the process of getting integrated into the kingdom of God involves, among other things, getting away from sin. That means repentance.

Repentance is a turning away from sin and a turning to God. It will mean undoing patterns of thought and behaviour which have been developed, perhaps over a long period of time. It may mean a whole change of lifestyle. We will have to appropriate to ourselves the new, often very different, patterns and lifestyle of the kingdom of God. The world's ways will no longer do.

Repentance is not just a single, distinct act, although it will certainly include many such distinct acts. It is more of an attitude, a way of relating to God and to others as well.

Repentance is not part of the world's agenda, not popular at all. It does not get a good press. And yet, it is the initial, essential, and introductory attitude or stance in the kingdom of God. It is both the entry point and the only way to stay in.

Jesus seems to reinforce this reality. The first recorded statement of his public ministry was: *"The kingdom of heaven is at hand. Repent and believe the good news"* (Mark 1:15).

The Church has consistently echoed this word. The popes of our own day have been particularly noteworthy in this regard. In his address Paenitemini of 1966, Pope Paul VI said: "We can reach the kingdom of God only by repentance, that *metanoia*, or conversion, which involves a radical, internal change of the whole human person." Pope John Paul II reiterated the same thought in his September 8, 1986 general audience when he said: "The message of repentance forms the very heart of the Church's mission."

Ongoing repentance will move us right to the centre of God's kingdom. It will move us from goodness to holiness. God is not satisfied with partial commitment. He is not satisfied with minimal standards. He is not content with those who simply observe the Commandments without striving to imitate his own total abandonment to the Father. He will not settle for anything less than a complete rejection of all that is alien to him, of all that separates us from the Father's love. He wants us to give him full permission to come into our lives and change our direction, our priorities, our plans, our attitudes, our hearts, minds, and souls. He will, through the powerful action of the Holy Spirit, transform the lives of those who surrender to him and live by his word.

It is very much out of style to talk about sin in today's world. We hear very little about it. Yet, that is what Jesus came to save us from. Sin is our biggest problem, both as a human society and as individuals. If sin could be called off altogether, human ills would virtually evaporate.

But the sense of sin has largely disappeared. Pope Pius XII put it this way: "The sin of the century," he said, "is the loss of the sense of sin" (*Message to the U.S. Catechetical Congress*, October 26, 1946). St. John says: *"If we say we have no sin, we deceive ourselves. The truth is not in us"* (1 John 1:8).

The Lord calls us to confront sin directly and to deal with it promptly. Otherwise, we get hurt. We get drawn away from God and his kingdom. The Lord wants us to face the reality of sin in our lives, not so that we will be defeated by it, but so that he can help us to experience victory over it.

Sin is exchanging the truth of God for a lie. It is worshipping and serving the creature instead of the Creator. It is exchanging the glory of God for the poor limitations of human nature. Sin is wresting control away from God.

A number of people object to repeated references to mankind's sinful condition. They say we are being too negative if we place any emphasis upon sin. We have to adopt a more positive approach, they insist. They suggest to us that the

Church talks too much about original sin. Is the Church not even hung up on sin? Why not concentrate rather on original blessing, a much more encouraging concept?

Sin is very negative alright. And if some talking about it can bring us to repentance, so much the better. Sweeping the reality of sin under the rug or denying it altogether is no help at all. As for the original blessing, it is long gone. But the Father has sent us a Saviour, the one through whom we can be blessed again.

If sin is the problem, repentance is the solution. Repentance is the first step away from sin and the first step toward holiness. We are called to holiness. God himself has said: "Be holy, for I am holy" (Lev 19:2). Jesus has challenged us in the same way. *"Be perfect,"* he has urged us, *"as your heavenly Father is perfect"* (Matt 5:48). We are to scale the cliffs of holiness, to climb the mountain of perfection. Repentance, a continual turning to the Lord, is to be the instrument of our ascent. It is for us to get on with the repentance we need.

Do we need any assistance? Are we not sure where to begin? The Lord is most eager to lend a helping hand. One of the requests he answers with a minimum of delay is the one that goes: 'Lord, if there's anything you want me to change in my life, would you please point it out?' The rapidity of the response will amaze us.

As to effective strategy, the 'divide and conquer' principle is best. Rather than try to take on every area of our lives at once, and probably be floored at the enormity of the task, it is advisable to ask the Lord to present us with just one project at a time. He is more than accommodating about this. He loves to see people shedding the shackles of sin and coming closer to him. He is seriously committed to providing all the help we need.

The Sacrament of Reconciliation is a vital tool in ongoing repentance. In it we celebrate the forgiveness Jesus has already won for us and apply it to our lives now. This sacramental encounter is an anointed moment in the life of believers. If we approach it with faith and expectation, we can experience healing from the roots of sin and begin to enter into a whole new freedom from the things that have been dragging us down.

Repentance may not always be easy, but it's very good for us. But, whatever the degree of difficulty, we must stay at it until it becomes a way of life.

Praise

The word 'praise' is actually generic. It encompasses three different responses to God: 1) thanksgiving, 2) praise, properly so termed, and 3) worship. The psalm-writer gives hint of this to some extent: *"Enter his gates with thanksgiving, his courts with praise"* (Ps 100:4). He is situating his teaching, of course, in the context of the temple. He is urging the people to offer to God the honour that is his due. They can utter phrases of thanksgiving as they enter, and sing songs of praise when they get inside.

Thanksgiving is rendering proper homage to God for the things that he has done. Praise is rendering him the same homage for who and what he is. Worship, as I see it, is the experience of being lifted up into the very life of the Trinity, being empowered by the Holy Spirit to speak the praises of Jesus to the glory of God the Father. This is Christian prayer in its highest form. If we persevere in giving thanks and praise to God, he may, at some point, take over and draw us to himself. This is worship. While our praise and thanksgiving are commanded by God and are simply our obedient response to his call, worship is something he gifts us to do. Praise and thanksgiving are largely the product of our own decision and effort. When we reach the point of worship, God takes over.

Some have asked: why does God command us to praise him? Does he need it? God, of course, does not need our recognition. He has, in fact, no needs at all. He calls us to praise him because he knows (having designed and created us) that it is something we need to do. If we don't give honour to God, we'll forget who we are. If we don't bow down before our Creator, we will begin to think we are in charge. It takes us a long time to learn that things in our lives do not work very well when we are in total control. Our lives come into good order and balance only when we give God his rightful place.

Praise is the best expression of my relationship with God. When I stand in praise of him, I am at my finest. Praise is a training ground for heaven. Praise will be the principal activity in the heavenly Jerusalem. Since my ultimate destiny is to be caught up in praise and worship of God, I might as well learn how to do it well here on earth and get started.

Jesus' disciples asked him to teach them how to pray (Luke 11:1). He responded with the formula that we have come to refer to as the Lord's Prayer. The phrase that follows our addressing God as "Father" is "hallowed be thy name." That's praise. Jesus is counselling them and us to give praise to God. It should not escape our notice either, that he places it right at the beginning. When we come to pray, he is saying, praise comes first.

Praise is meant to come first every time we pray, whether in private or together. The focus of this particular piece is prayer in common.

When we praise God together, we join our voices in common acclaim. We sing the songs that give him honour and we glorify his name with spontaneous words and tunes. The volume of our homage can rise and fall as we strive to be sensitive to the promptings of the Holy Spirit and to be led by him.

How loud should we be? My voice should be loud enough so that those nearest me can hear me and be encouraged by my efforts, but I should not be at such volume as to drown them out. We should all be taking our cue from the one who is leading. We will be very loud at times, even to the point of a joyful shout, and our voices will be very soft and quiet at other times.

The enthusiasm with which I enter into the time of praise

should not depend on how I feel. It is a decision that I simply put into action no matter what. I don't really think the Lord is at all impressed with a person who says: "I just couldn't get into it today. I didn't feel like it."

Spontaneous praise is for everybody. It isn't an exercise for extroverts. It isn't a peculiar form of spirituality. It isn't just for members of the charismatic movement. It has nothing whatever to do with emotions. It is a very Catholic form of common prayer, one that, though not very common experience today, has a very real place in the history of the Church. It is something the Lord is restoring to his people in our day. It is something the Companions of the Cross endorse and practise with great conviction and purpose.

Our times of praise will normally include some of what is called 'singing in the Spirit'. This will draw each one present into spontaneous melodies in any language and often, if truly being led by the Spirit of God, will result in very striking harmonies. This, too, finds its place in Catholic experience. (For an excellent historical examination of this phenomenon, read Eddie Ensley's little book, Sounds of Wonder.) People may sing in the Spirit in any language, even in a prayer language the Lord might give. It has been called 'jubilation' by numerous authors of the past, including St. Augustine (*Enarrationes in Psalmos*, 32).

Our praise will usually lead us into silence, into a time of listening to the Lord. Those present may feel led to share insights, Scripture references, words that just might be from God.

Praise is a human activity. It obviously involves the use of our voices. But it is meant to be a much more complete human activity. We can raise our hands. Scripture is rich with references to the raising of the hands to God. The psalmist says: *"To you, O Lord, I lift up my hands"* (Ps 28:2). The prayer of the Liturgy of the Hours, the Church's official prayer, for Tuesday evening, week 1, reads: "May this lifting up of our hands in prayer be a sacrifice pleasing in your sight." The Lord can be applauded. Once again the psalmist speaks: *"All you peoples, clap your hands. Shout to God with cries of gladness"* (Ps 47:2). We can bow down or kneel. *"All the people ... bowed low, prostrating themselves to the ground"* (Neh 8:6). *"Paul knelt down with them all and prayed"* (Acts 20:36). We can even dance. *"David danced before the Lord with abandon"* (2 Sam 6:14).

Praise of God, praise rising to him from loyal hearts, hands, and voices, puts evil spirits to rout. They can't stand it. Listen to St. Ignatius of Antioch: "Try to gather more often to give yourselves to God and to praise him. For, when you do this, Satan's powers are undermined and his plans are thwarted" (*Letter to the Ephesians*).

Praise moves us from a response to God's command to a response to God's anointing. As we continue to focus upon the Lord and give him all the honour and reverence he deserves, we can be overtaken by an anointing of the Holy Spirit that will draw us into a deeper experience of God's presence, into a time of worship, a time that may be characterized by revelation, words from the Lord, insights, convictions, consolations from him.

Genuine praise and worship will work change in our lives. We simply will not be able to come before the Lord on any kind of regular basis without coming more and more into his order. Patterns of sin just have to begin releasing their hold on our lives.

Like so many other things, praise begins as a decision, becomes a skill that we learn, and ends as a gift from God. Like nothing else, it brings us closer and closer to God.

Prayer

One of the things that, very early in their travels with Jesus, fascinated the disciples was his commitment to personal prayer, something they knew only a little about. They did not really know who he was, but they were extremely impressed with him. He was so strong and consistent. He had such inner peace. He spoke such powerful words. He performed such amazing signs. He was so evidently a man of God, a prophet for sure, perhaps even in the line of the great prophets like Moses, Elijah, and Elisha. They were quite sure that there was a connection between what he said and did on the one hand and his time of quiet prayer on the other.

So, they asked him about it. He responded by giving them the formula we have come to know as the Lord's Prayer and by other directions as well. If we want to know how to pray well, we can do no better than to learn from Jesus himself.

We can find no better definition for prayer, I think, than the one the old catechisms gave: Prayer is the raising of the mind and heart to God. It is a communication with God. Jesus kept in regular touch with his Father while he was on earth. Luke says: *"Then he went out to the mountain to pray, spending the night in communion with God"* (Luke 6:12). Communication, or communion, is a two-way exercise. It involves both talking and listening. We can pour out our hearts to the Lord and tell him everything we can think of, but if we want to give him a chance to speak, we will have to fall silent for a while and listen.

If we are going to pray well, we are going to have to find a quiet place. Jesus says: *"When you pray, go into your private room and close the door"* (Matt 6:6). Are our lives so shared with other people and so hectic that we have serious trouble finding a spot remote enough to make prayer possible? If so, my feeling is that the Lord would be most happy to arrange something for us if we tell him we're serious about getting down to some regular quiet prayer.

Each person has to make the decision as to when is the best time to get alone with God. Jesus has something to say about that, however: *"Rising early the next morning, he went off to a lonely place in the desert; there, he was absorbed in prayer"* (Mark 1:35). Jesus' days tended to be very full. In order to get some regular quality time with his Father, he made the only possible choice. He got up early. Do I hear somebody saying:

"I can't do it. I'm just not a morning person"? Somehow, I don't think the Lord is too impressed with this testimony. Getting up in the morning is a decision, not a gift, and not a personality trait. If the only really workable time I can find for prayer is the early morning, the Lord's word is clear: Get up!

It is good to be as spontaneous as possible in prayer with the Lord, to speak to him in our words rather than in somebody else's. But, at the same time, some kind of structure or procedure will be helpful. Different programs will work for different people. Here is one that I find works most of the time for me:

1. **Thanksgiving.** The psalm writer suggests that we *"enter his gates with thanksgiving"* (Ps 100:4). I begin by thanking God for or in all the events of the previous 24 hours. I thank him for all the good things and thank him in all the things that weren't so good. St. Paul says that, *"all things work together unto good for those who love God"* (Rom 8:28). As we consciously turn everything over to the Lord, he is able to draw forth his purposes.

2. **Repentance.** This will again require going over the day before. It is important for us to 'own' our sins, to acknowledge them before God, to repudiate them, and to tell the Lord we are going to take whatever steps are necessary to avoid them. This makes our repentance effective.

3. **Forgiveness.** Jesus again and again urged forgiveness. He said: *"Whenever you stand in prayer, forgive"* (Mark 11:25). Some people find this difficult. It shouldn't be. They say their feelings get in the way. They don't 'feel' like forgiving somebody in particular. The Lord wants us to know that forgiveness is not a feeling. It's a decision. As we take people before the Lord quietly in prayer and tell him we want to forgive them, God is freed up to deal with our feelings. It is good, too, from time to time, to ask the Lord to reveal to us anybody we still haven't really forgiven.

He's very good at popping names and faces into our heads.

4. **Praise.** The decks should now be cleared for us to give glory to God. We can use every word or phrase we can think of to render the honour to him that is his due. When words in our own native tongue seem to run dry, we can just make up sounds, something he can turn into the little gift of tongues. We can sing songs or make up little tunes of our own. Praise is a very active form of prayer. There is no listening here. It is good for us to really turn it on at this point. Praise takes us entirely out of ourselves and turns us fully to God.

5. **The Holy Spirit.** I now invite the Holy Spirit to do his work. I tell him the red carpet is down for him to move in and accomplish the Father's purposes. The Holy Spirit's main work is bringing forth the kingdom of God. I give him leave to do it in me, in all those with whom I am in relationship, and in the tasks the Father has assigned to me within the Church.

6. **Rebuking.** In the realm of the spirit, it's the Holy Spirit I want or the angels of God sent in Jesus' name by the Father. I'm not interested in any others. I want no truck or trade with spirits of evil. Because we live in a sinful world, they can, however, harass us. Jesus tells us to do what he has done. He rebuked the evil spirits and drove them away. He says: *"I have given you power to tread upon snakes and scorpions"* (Luke 10:19). St. Paul puts it this way: *"The weapons of our warfare are mighty. With them, we have power to pull down strongholds"* (2 Cor 10:4). That all seems quite clear. So, I rebuke them and, in Jesus' name, command them to go. The ones I give attention to are division, rebellion, confusion, deception, criticism, doubt, disbelief, secularism, materialism, worldliness, lust, anger, pride, and fear. I don't waste a lot of time with this, but I do include it.

7. **I then will invite the Lord to take over in my life completely.** I will consciously give him all I am and have. I specifically include my positions, my priorities, my plans, and my possessions. I opt for the stewardship system Jesus calls for. He becomes the owner. I do his bidding. I tell him I want to surrender to him completely.
8. **This is not a gift.** It is something we must decide to do. As we make the decision, the Lord strengthens us with his grace. It is particularly important for us to tell the Lord we are trusting in him on the bad days, the days when everything seems to have messed up, the times when we see no way out of some dilemma, in all trials of whatever kind.
9. **Availability.** I will renew here my daily offer. I will tell the Lord that, whatever he might have in mind for me, I will do it. Or, if he happens to have some plan on the go and can't find anybody to take it on, I'll tell him I'm available. This one has got me into trouble a few times, but I'm convinced it's what God wants.
10. **Scripture.** I will ask the Lord to lead me to some places in the Bible which may be important for me to read right now and, having read them, sit back and ponder over them. This will involve me in the listening time of my prayer. I will wait upon the Lord for a while.
11. **Journal.** If anything has occurred to me, I will jot it down in my log book. Going back over this from time to time is a good way to check up on what the Lord has been, perhaps, saying to me and how he may have been leading me.
12. **Petition.** I customarily finish my quiet time with the Lord by placing intentions before him.

This is what I have become accustomed to doing during my quiet time with the Lord. This is not my only time of prayer for the day, however. I celebrate the Eucharist, pray the Divine Office (some of it with the brothers of the household), and get in five of the mysteries of the Rosary.

The structure I use for my personal prayer time usually works reasonably well for me, but I have learned that the Lord wants me to be flexible enough to change it to suit his particular purposes for any given day. It may involve leaving out some, many, or all, of my carefully constructed sections.

In any case, God wants a commitment from me to spend daily time with him. It is only in this way that he can effectively deal with me, straighten me out when I need it, and keep me reasonably on track. Jesus calls us into friendship with him, with the Father, and with the Holy Spirit. To be friends, we have to spend time together.

Obedience

If virtues were to be rated according to their popularity, obedience would be near the bottom of the ladder. We live in a day when the principle of "doing one's own thing" has been canonized. Taking orders is definitely out of style.

Most of us, I would think, have little trouble with the authority of God. But, when he wants to exercise it through others?—major problem!

It probably has something to do with the experience many, virtually all, of us have had with the way authority has been exercised over us. Perhaps it was inconsistent or overly-demanding parents. It may have been the school system or heavy-handed teachers. Or maybe an impersonal work place. Ladder-climbing bosses can be a severe trial. We may even have been chewed up a bit within the Church. In any case, few of us have come through unscathed.

Nonetheless, the Lord is calling us to be obedient, not only to him, but to those placed over us.

I have heard it said that we need obey someone in authority only when he/she is 'in the Lord'. Not so. We are not free to pick and choose whom we shall obey. If a person is lawfully set over us, we have no choice. We are to obey. A favourite set of Scriptures for those who would prefer to choose is found in the Acts of the Apostles. Peter and John, in appearing before the Sanhedrin, said to them: *"Judge for yourselves whether it be right in God's sight for us to obey you rather than God"* (Acts 4:19). *During a second appearance, Peter told the same body:* *"Better for us to obey God than men"* (Acts 5:29). But this has to be seen in its proper context. At the time the apostles were being harassed by this august body, the Lord had taken the mantle of authority from the Sanhedrin and placed it upon none other than the apostles themselves. Had the confrontation occurred a couple of months earlier, Peter and John and the others would have had to obey.

There are a couple of other Scriptures that are more *ad rem*. Jesus himself said a most unusual thing one day. Speaking to the crowds and to his disciples at the same time, he told them: *"The scribes and the Pharisees occupy the chair of Moses. Therefore, you must listen to what they say and do what they tell you. Do not, however, imitate their example"* (Matt 23:2). The reference to the chair of Moses has to do with authority. Unworthy though those in authority may be, they are to be obeyed. That's God's way. If we follow it, he will bless it.

The author of the letter to the Hebrews, dealing with the same subject, puts it this way: *"You must obey your leaders and submit to them, for it is their appointed task to have care over you, and they must, in their turn, render due account"* (Heb 13:17). The duty, it would seem, of those in authority is to exercise proper care for those under them. They will be assessed on that basis. For those under authority, what God expects of them is clear. They are to be obedient.

The Lord has set up the Church with some very clear lines of authority. For most of us, bishops and pastors, along with legitimately appointed superiors, are the ones we are to obey. (It is understood, of course, we are absolved of our duty to obey if we are told to do something sinful.)

If we are convinced of the truth of all this, it remains simply for us to make a decision to obey and to follow through with it. An effective decision should take care of it.

Not so simple. The human factor continues to intervene. We still have trouble with authority. We can find any number of reasons not to obey. The authority person is unreasonable. Or he is uninformed. Or he doesn't know what he's doing. Or his track record is poor. Or, surely, the Lord doesn't want me to obey in this particular situation. The authority/obedience combination is truly a problem. But the problem is not with the authority person, whatever his shortcomings. The problem is with the one who won't obey.

I was trying to punch this point home in a homily not so long ago. Afterwards, a young university student thought he would offer a comment on the message. He gave me to understand in no uncertain terms that he thought I was way off the mark. "Look at all the great things that have been done throughout history by people who were disobeying the authorities." My only rejoinder was to the effect that if they had obeyed, they probably would have done even greater things. I think I was right. But, all the same, obedience is just not a very popular virtue.

I believe most of our problems with authority would disappear if only we could see it, not as a privilege or as an exercise of power, but as a gift.

Obedience is God's way. Could there be a better example than Jesus himself? He said: *"My food is to do the will of the one who sent me"* (John 4:34). Jesus obeyed. In fact, he was obedient unto death. Did the Father bless his obedience? Jesus' death was the cause of the opening of the gates of life, the salvation of the whole world. Jesus' obedience was very richly blessed.

Making the decision to obey requires a large measure of trust from us. We have to learn to trust the Lord to work out his purposes through the structures that he himself has established. Our decision to obey should be without strings attached. It should be to obey the Lord no matter what he chooses to speak, in whatever way he chooses to speak it, before we ever know what it might be. That's the kind of obedience he likes. That's the kind of obedience he will richly bless.

The strategy the Lord wants us to follow seems plain to me. He wants us to obey. He wants us to lift our superiors up in prayer and to trust him to work through them.

As for me, I made a personal decision some years ago to be obedient in all things to my lawful superior, my bishop. I can only say that, though it has not always been easy, it has always been blessed. I have freely given up the luxury of pledging to obey the bishop provided what he was telling me to do agreed with what I thought the Holy Spirit was saying to me. It's been obedience first, last, and always.

Still, obedience is just not 'in' these days, even in the Church. It is a very unpopular virtue. Too bad. I can't help feeling what a powerful revival could start in the Church if only we'd obey.

Fasting

The will of God seems clear about fasting. He likes it. And he honours it as well.

The Old Testament is replete with references to fasting, both individual and corporate. Again and again, in times of trouble, the leaders of the people would call for a fast. The prophet Joel issued a striking summons. *"Blow the trumpet in Zion!"* he proclaimed. *"Proclaim a fast. Call an assembly. Gather the people. Notify the congregation. Assemble the elders. Bring the children, even infants at the breast"* (Joel 2:15-16).

Things didn't change when Jesus came to earth. He fasted himself. When he was led out to the desert to be tempted, *"he fasted forty days and forty nights"* (Matt 4:2). He took it for granted that people would undertake an occasional or even regular fast. He gave counsel about it. *"When you fast,"* he told them, *"do not look gloomy the way the hypocrites do. They change the expressions on their faces so that others may know they are fasting. They are already repaid, I assure you. But when you fast, have your hair groomed and your face washed.*

That way, nobody will know you are fasting except your Father whom you do not see. And your Father, who sees all things done in secret, will repay you" (Matt 6:16-18).

It does indeed seem clear. The Lord wants us to fast. He wants us to do it without fanfare. And he honours it. That should surely be enough for us. If God wants it, we'll do it. But it would probably help if we understood it.

Jesus was quite ready, not only to call for it, but to explain it. One day, some of John the Baptist's disciples put a question to him about it. *"Why is it,"* they asked, *"that, while both we and the Pharisees fast, your disciples do not?"* Jesus' response gives us the clue we're looking for. *"But surely the wedding guests would not fast,"* he replied, *"as long as the bridegroom was with them. As long as he is present, they would not fast. The day will come, however, when the bridegroom is taken away from them. On that day they will fast"* (Mark 2:18:20).

So that's it, then. The purpose of fasting is to be in touch with the bridegroom. When we fast, we are able to be in better communication with the Lord. We do not fast in order to fast. We fast in order to pray. All other things being equal, prayer is more effective when accompanied by a fast than it is without it.

Father Slavko Barbaric, OFM, of Medjugorje, puts it this way in his book, *Fasting*: "Fasting will lead us to a new freedom of heart and mind. By fasting, we detach our hearts from the good things that tie us to the affairs of this world."

In our day, fasting has largely gone out of fashion. Outside the context of trying to lose weight, most people simply do not fast.

Many will be able to remember when fasting was mandated by the Church. During the weekdays of Lent, all Catholics between the ages of 21 and 65 were enjoined to fast. The instructions from Church authorities were to the effect that one full meal a day was allowed with two meals of lesser quantity which together amounted to less than the big one. My strategy was to make sure to include one whopper of a meal each day so that the other two could be of more or less regular size and the pangs of hunger could be staved off. I'm not too sure how meritorious my fasting was. At any rate, when the fasting rules were lifted, that was the end of it for me. I suspect I wasn't the only one.

I think we can probably do better than that. If we are serious about growing in our relationship with the Lord, we will have to include some fasting.

When the Medjugorje[1] word on fasting reached us a few years ago (bread and water only every Friday—all 24 hours of it), many people charged into it with willing hearts. The results were interesting. Coffee addicts got blasting headaches that rendered them all but dysfunctional. One religious sister told me she got so weak she couldn't walk. She had to crawl to the bathroom on her hands and knees. Another woman explained her system of dealing with it. She would have a huge meal very late Thursday and then try to sleep all day Friday. Saturday morning breakfast was becoming the highlight of many people's weeks. Early. Very early.

I stayed with it as long as I could. I eventually got to the point where I would stay up 'till midnight Friday, then stuff out. There I would be at a few minutes to 12, sandwich prepared and glass of milk poured, waiting it out. At the stroke of midnight, I'd get into it and invariably eat too much.

Something had to give. People were getting discouraged about their inability to live up to it, feeling guilty, but quietly giving the whole thing up entirely.

Somewhat consoling words came out of the same Medjugorje a bit later. Not everybody can handle the same kind of fast. Each one has to seek out what's possible for him/her.

Certain things have become evident. To be effective, the fast we undertake has to be regular. It can't be something that compromises our capacity to carry out our ordinary duties.

---

[1] This is a private revelation and the Companions of the Cross will abide by any official judgments of the Church regarding it.

It ordinarily has to do with giving up food and drink in some way, but it doesn't have to be. For people who are unable to tamper with their food programs, other ways of fasting are possible. They can fast from television, from radio, from newspapers. Voluntarily pulling away from things we ordinarily depend on can work to allow us to depend more on God, to be in closer touch with him. In other words, we can pray better.

Fasting needs to make a comeback. We have lots to pray for.

Journaling

A lot of people shy away from the suggestion that they should consider keeping personal journals. It must be because they misunderstand what's involved. Or maybe these are the people who once tried to maintain diaries and found they couldn't stay with it. A journal is not a diary.

A spiritual journal is related to my time of personal prayer, my daily quiet time with the Lord. Whatever writing I decide to do in it can ordinarily be done during prayer time. In fact, many people refer to these little notebooks as their prayer journals.

To my prayer journal I can commit my promises to the Lord. I can write in my requests. I can thank him for blessings, for specific answers to petitions. I can summarize my day, include reflections on what I sense God may be saying to me, and record resolutions I make as to how I should respond. I can register my complaints. Among the things I think I've learned about the Lord is that he likes me to complain to him. He doesn't want me to complain to others, but he likes to give me the chance to get things off my chest in conversation with him. He can handle it. Even if I'm a bit angry with him, he doesn't mind my writing that down either. He is totally unthreatened by my annoyance. He knows allowing me to express it can be quite therapeutic for me. All of these things and more I can record in my journal.

It may sound like a lot, but it really isn't. Five minutes a day should take care of it. Some days maybe nothing needs to be written.

The value of the prayer journal is, perhaps, two-fold: writing things down may help me to get my thoughts into focus, and keeping a record of how my relationship with the Lord is progressing can be a very useful reminder as time goes on.

We are all eager to catch the Lord's word. We want to know what he is saying to us. Very often, as we continue to pursue his will, we forget what he has already said. If we are faithful to journaling, we'll have the record we need. I get the impression God doesn't say everything at once. Probably to keep us seeking him, he will give us his word a bit at a time. If we don't keep a record of it, we are liable to forget it.

It is useful, I find, in writing in my journal, to address God in the first person. I write directly to him, to the Father. That way, it keeps me in prayer, keeps me communicating with him.

Over the past few years, I have been reasonably faithful to the practice of keeping a journal. There were a couple of extended periods, however, when I just let it go and didn't bother. I have lived to regret it. I have looked back on those unrecorded times and wondered again and again what was happening in my life. I can't remember. I've lost it.

In order to make journaling most effective, I have to do a regular review. Every couple of months serves to keep me up to date.

A journal well kept will be like a folio of personal correspondence with the Lord. Keeping such a record can be a very valuable help to anyone who wants to grow into a closer union with him.

Feelings and Discernment

We have a strong conviction that God himself has plans for his people and will convey them to us if we ask. The process of trying to get hold of his plan can be very difficult. It is not supposed to be so. But, our experience is that it often poses quite a challenge. Our further conclusion is that the source of the difficulty lies in the way we seek the word from him. As St. James says: *"The reason you do not get what you are asking for is that you are not praying in the right way"* (Jas 4:3).

We, of course, are anxious to get it right. We know that it is God's plan that will work best and that, in fact, his will is really the only thing worth doing at all.

We have many decisions to make as we pilgrim forward with the Lord. The men who are pursuing a possible call to the priesthood have an obvious decision to come to. Those who are discerning marriage or the celibate state are likewise engaged in the same pursuit. But there are many other things that call for choices: school matters, family decisions, work directions. These are but a few.

Many factors tend to influence our decisions in one way or other. The one that most often causes difficulty is our feelings. God usually will speak his word in our hearts, and we will recognize it by the peace that goes with it. The problem is that we tend to confuse peace with feeling good. We have to be able to distinguish between peace and good feelings. "If it feels good, do it," is a teaching that comes from the world, not from God. Feelings have a definite purpose in the plan of God, but they are most unreliable as factors in discernment. God's peace is most reliable.

I can have true peace about something I think the Lord is showing me and, at the same time, not feel very good about it at all. Provided I am meeting the conditions for hearing the Lord correctly, the peace that he gives me enables me to say: "I just know it's right." I may not feel too great about it, but I know it's right.

The world does everything by feelings. In fact, it is preoccupied with feelings. We live in the world and are bound to be affected by it, though Jesus did say we were not to be *"of the world"* (John 17:16). We have to know that it is very possible for us to get too involved with our feelings. Discernment is more than getting in touch with my feelings.

Marriage partner decisions today are, of course, based upon feelings. This may not be working too well. Modern marriage is in serious trouble. Love is as much a decision, and a daily one at that, as it is a feeling. The spouse I'm looking for needs to be the one the Lord wants to lead me to, not the one I'm "falling in love" with right now. Our experience tells that we can fall in and out of love, and back in, many different times and with many different people.

It may sound as though we are teaching that feelings are of no value, or that we must deny them, or that there is no point in taking them into account. Quite the contrary. Feelings are extremely valuable. We just have to try to understand how they work. While they are not very good discernment factors, they are excellent signals for us. They tell us where we're at, not where to go. They can give us warning, tell us what to avoid. If it's anger or hatred we are feeling, we will have to be careful what we do or say about it.

Our feelings are not our enemies. They are not sinful. It is not a sin to feel emotions. It is as natural to hate as it is to love. The sin is in how we treat the people we have bad feelings about. We must not deny our feelings. We must face them and find some effective way of dealing with them.

But, we must not base decisions upon how we feel. The reason they are not reliable in this way is two-fold: the general woundedness (from sin) of human nature, and the constant brainwashing about feelings that we get from the world. It has an effect upon us whether we like it or not.

The transforming action of the Holy Spirit, his power to heal, will have, as one of its objectives, the healing of my emotions. If we allow him, the Lord will work within us to bring our feelings into line so that they, more and more, will instinctively support his word within us. Some people are farther along the road to wholeness than others. That's just the way it is. It is important for each of us to know where we stand.

Our feelings are meant to be great assets to us. But they

are not to be factors in discernment. God's peace is what we need. It is a priceless gift. It produces deep conviction within me, and I will know when I have it.

Simplicity of Life

This is one of the basic components of the vision we felt that God was giving us back in the spring of 1985. The Companions of the Cross were to embrace some kind of simple lifestyle. It was probably the part of the vision with which we were the least comfortable. We're still not sure exactly what the Lord means by it, but we have an unsettling sense that he will make it clear to us as we go along. It will be for us to live it out and to do it without compromise.

The call of the Gospel is plain enough. Simplicity of life is expected of all real disciples of Jesus. I have long been uneasy with the so-called prosperity gospel, the teaching that, when we turn our lives over to the Lord, he will shower material blessings upon us. As much as I'd like to believe it, it just doesn't wash. Of course, I'm just as uneasy with the word on simplicity, but I simply can't deny the authentic ring that it has.

Jesus says of himself: *"The Son of Man has nowhere to lay his head"* (Matt 8:20). He was cautioning those who were getting ready to make the decision to become his disciples. He was telling them that it wasn't going to be easy, that there would be a cost involved, and that the cost was total. To become his followers would cost them everything. Jesus had no real home to call his own, had no income, no insurance policies, nothing the world we live in would demand by way of elementary security. He was even buried in a borrowed grave.

He says: *"Do not worry about your livelihood, what you are to eat or drink or use for clothing. Is not life more than food? Is not the body more valuable than clothes? Look at the birds in the sky. They do not sow or reap; they gather nothing into barns. Yet your heavenly Father feeds them.*

Are you not more important than they? Which of you by worrying can add a moment to his life-span? As for clothes, why be concerned? Learn a lesson from the way the wild flowers grow. They do not work; they do not spin. Yet, I assure you, not even Solomon in all his splendour was arrayed like one of these. If God can clothe in such splendour the grass of the field, which blooms today and is thrown on the fire tomorrow, will he not provide much more for you?" (Matt 6:25-30). Does it sound as though Jesus wants his followers to live uncomplicated lives, lives unencumbered by a concern for the goods of this world and characterized by a very total trust in God?

He asks, too, a very pointed question: *"What does it profit a man to gain the whole world and suffer the loss of his own immortal soul?"* (Mark 8:36). The answer to the question is 'zero'. It profits us nothing to 'make it' in this world if eternal life should slip from our grasp. Jesus is telling us to keep it simple.

Jesus' message is at complete odds with the teaching of the world. The word we hear around us day in and day out is 'Get secure. Pile up as many possessions as you can. Money may not be everything, but it can certainly buy everything.' To this, Jesus says: *"Get purses for yourselves that do not wear out, a neverfailing treasure with the Lord which no thief comes near nor any moth destroys"* (Luke 12:33). Of course, he was speaking of the kingdom of God. *"Seek first,"* he urges us, *"the kingdom of God"* (Matt 6:33).

His well-known word—*"It is easier for a camel to pass through a needle's eye than for a rich man to enter the kingdom of God"* (Mt 19:24)—seems to leave little room for guesswork as to what he is saying about the lifestyle that befits a follower of his.

If we are to be honest with ourselves, we are going to have to conclude, I am convinced, that the material standards by which we in the Western world live are unrealistic and probably immoral.

A few years ago, I read a report stating that 87% of the

world's resources were being consumed by 14% of the world's population. The report included a prediction that, by the 1990's, a greater percentage of resources would be required, at the present rate of development, by a smaller percentage of people. In 1981, the United States of America alone, comprising a mere 6% of the population of the world, consumed 33% of the world's resources. These statistics, as we know, refer to us in the so-called first world. This has to be turned around. It is a situation that cries to heaven for redress. We ourselves have to do something about it. It means, for all of us in the 'have' nations, moving to simpler and simpler standards of living. Somebody is going to have to lead the way. Are the Companions of the Cross to be somewhere in the vanguard? We think so.

There is a strong and consistent New Testament word about money. Saint Paul writes to Timothy: *"If we have food and clothing, we have all we need. Those who want to be rich are falling into temptation and a trap. They are letting themselves be captured by foolish and harmful desires which drag men down to ruin and destruction. The love of money is the root of all evil. Some men, in their passion for it, have strayed from the faith and have come to grief amid great pain"* (1 Tim 6:8-10). Again, we read: *"Do not love money, but be content with what you have. For God has said—'I will never desert you, nor will I forsake you'"* (Heb 13:5). It is an echo of the same message from the Old Testament. *"The just man's few possessions,"* the psalmist assures us, *"are better than the wicked man's wealth"* (Ps 37:16). The word is a challenge for us all.

Of the many prophets the Lord has provided for his people in our day, few speak the simplicity word as well as Jean Vanier. Here are some words from his book, *The Broken Body*:

"Never before have we been so aware of the immense gap between those who have and those who have not. The poor are mainly in the southern hemisphere where the population is growing; but they are also in the slums of every city, out of work. Others are locked up in institutions and hospitals.

The rich get richer, holding onto their power, their prestige and their privileges, increasingly afraid of and disturbed by the poor, frightened of facing a reality which calls for change" (p. 9).

"...many people do not know how to rest. They are like rolling locomotives, fuelled by anguish, and perhaps by the fear of stopping ... Each one of us must find our own secret rhythm of how to rest, relax, and find recreation, for each one of our bodies is different. We need personal space and time ... If we are just doers, feeling terribly responsible and serious, we will crack up one day. We must nourish the passive part of us, our hearts made for a personal love, learning to listen to others, to marvel at nature, to rest a moment in the presence of Jesus, to receive the presence of those around us and be nourished by their trust, enjoying the little things of each day, not taking ourselves too seriously, accepting to become like little children" (p. 120).

And he doesn't just talk about it. He does it.

Actually, for those of us who are ordained, there is no option. The law of the Church tells us we are to live relatively simple lives. "Clerics are to follow a simple way of life and avoid anything which smacks of worldliness" (*The Code of Canon Law,* canon 282.1).

Vatican II speaks to the clergy as well. "With special care, they should be so trained in priestly obedience, poverty, and a spirit of self-denial, that they may accustom themselves to living in conformity with the crucified Christ and to giving up willingly even those things which are lawful but not expedient" (*Optatam Totius,* 9).

But it is easy to generalise. What we have to do is find ways to make the clear teaching of Jesus to his disciples and his well-discerned word to the Companions of the Cross into workable, day to day principles of living. We do not feel we as yet have the full directions of the Lord on the matter, but we can certainly make a start. Here are five areas we can have a look at:

1. Tithing

God's Old Testament people had some very concrete commands from him about what they were to contribute to his work. It was 10% of everything. And that meant 10% of their gross. Off the top. There is no record that Jesus ever abrogated this teaching. In fact, he urged people to even greater generosity. The early Church went even further. The earliest Christians made a radical commitment to share all things in common.[2]

I am convinced God still wants his tithe. A few years ago, having heard this word and prayed about it, I felt I could stall no longer. I took a deep breath and began to tithe. I have to testify that it has brought great blessings into my life. Whereas, before I started to do it, I was barely scraping by on a month to month basis, once I was into it, my bank balance was always quite sufficient. I think the Lord wants us to know that there is a promise attached to it. He doesn't commit himself to making us rich, but he does intend to take care

of us. What tithing has done for me is to make it possible for me to stop being concerned about how I'm going to manage materially and allow me to concentrate more fully on the Lord himself.

I am convinced the Lord wants it of us. I would urge all Companions of the Cross and lay associates who are not doing so, to take a deep breath and to plunge into the fascinating world of the tithe. It's like getting ducked in cool water on a warm day. It's great once we get in.

---

[2] Fr. Bob is speaking here of those with economic security. He fully accepted the teaching of the Catholic Church that "no one is commanded to distribute to others that which is required for his own necessities and those of his household; nor even to give away what is reasonably required to keep up becomingly his condition in life; 'for no one ought to live unbecomingly'. But when necessity has been supplied, and one's position fairly considered, it is a duty to give to the indigent out of that which is over" (Pope Leo XIII, *Rerum Novarum*, 22).

2. *Almsgiving*

Jesus did not do away with the tithe. He seemed to encourage even going well beyond it. He called for a degree of generosity that virtually all of us are totally unfamiliar with.

I learned a lesson about generosity some years ago. When I was first ordained, my assignment was to a parish which already had two other priests, the pastor and another assistant, the latter being a few years older than I. Both were generous, but my fellow assistant was clearly the most generous person I have ever met. He almost literally gave everything away. He gave money to all who came begging to the rectory door. He gave his clothes away to those who needed them. One day, he even gave his car away. He was something like a depot with money and goods coming in and going out all the time. But the Lord took care of him. People were always giving him money. Shortly after his car had gone, someone came by unexpectedly and gave him another car, better than the one he had given away. I'm not sure exactly how the whole thing worked, but this I know: it did work.

How generous are we? When was the last time I gave something away?

3. *Owning, Using, and Sharing*

I think the Lord wants us to settle the ownership question. Being a disciple of Jesus includes, among other things, making everything over to him. I don't own things any more. I manage them for him. I become what the Gospels call a steward.

I should follow a carefully planned and approved budget. I have to know where my money is going and how it is being spent. I have to know how to handle the advertising and marketing strategies the media are blowing at me every day. I can't let myself get brainwashed into believing I have to have every new gadget. I have to realize that industries are manufacturing goods with a carefully designed obsolescence factor built in. My purchases should reflect a wisdom that understands the deceptions we all face. Impulse buying, of course, has to go. We must bring into submission every desire that is centred in greed.

Our houses and our personal rooms should reflect the Gospel we preach. We should keep only those things that are necessary for us to live decently and to carry out the work the Lord has given us. They should be presentable and clean.

Our clothing should be reasonable in style, masculine in appearance, and free from vanity and ostentation.

Part of living a simple lifestyle means being willing to lend things to one another. This can be a sensitive area. Living under the cloud of original sin, we can get very possessive about the things that are ours. Supposing somebody puts a scratch on my car or misplaces one of my books or my tapes? I think I can hear the Lord saying: 'So what! Is it really that important?'

What am I going to say the next time one of my brothers or sisters asks to borrow something?

4. Living together

One of the things I felt most sure of a few years ago was that God was telling me to share my dwelling. Living with others, brothers in my case, is a great way to simplify one's life. There is less temptation to complicate my life with things I really don't need.

I can much more easily share my time and my goods.

Living together will necessarily entail my giving up a good measure of my privacy, too. Perhaps a whole study should be launched among us as to how much private space the Lord wants us to have. We might even listen carefully to people from some communities who feel that the sharing of rooms can serve the brothers' way of life in many ways.

Living together is not easy. It takes a lot of effort to make it work. But I'm convinced it's the Lord's way. It's worth the effort it takes.

Am I sure my present living arrangements are the ones the

Lord wants me to have? Am I willing to change them?

5. General lifestyle

When I eat out, where do I go? Will Bert's Beanery do, or does it always have to be the El Trocadero? Must I have so many clothes, or always buy such high quality? What kind of car do I drive? How dedicated am I to gadgetry? Must I have the latest energy-saving device? Am I into exotic holidays?

I think the Lord would have us hear closely the words of Jesus to Martha: *"You are concerned about too many things. Only one is necessary"* (Luke 10:41-42). What is the one thing Jesus wants us to get concerned about? Following him—that's what he wants.

We don't want to be like the seed that fell upon the footpath. *"It was choked by life's worries, riches, and pleasures. It did not take root"* (Luke 8:14).

I think the Lord wants us to know that the more we have, the more we will have to worry about.

We, the Companions of the Cross, are to be a society of apostolic life when the Lord opens the door for this to happen. We are thus not enjoined to what is known as evangelical poverty, the lifestyle where nobody owns anything in his own right, where everybody contributes all he has and receives what he needs. But, we are very clear about his call to simplicity. We have to search out its full implications carefully and, as we gain what will probably be a gradual understanding of God's plan on our behalf, we will have to be scrupulous about living it.

The Lord is speaking to us about lifestyle. He wants some changes. We're not sure yet just what all those changes might wind up being. But if we're giving him the green light to lead us wherever he wants us to go, he'll move us to the simplicity he wants for us. When I'm tempted to avoid the issue, to feel that maybe this whole simplicity business is not so important after all, I think I hear Jesus' words: *"Wherever your treasure lies, there your heart will be"* (Luke 12:34).

Tithing

The Father's plan to save his people has been to send his Son to earth to become one of us, to take our sins upon himself, and to bear them to the Cross. With the death of Jesus, eternal salvation became a possibility for everyone. On our part, entering personally into that salvation involves repentance and making Jesus Lord.

Our faith, of which our religion is the expression, is essentially, first and foremost, a relationship with a person, the person of Jesus Christ. We are called, for sure, to be members of his Church and to place our lives in his order. But our relationship with him comes first. It is the Father's desire that Jesus be Lord of each one's life.

Making Jesus my only Lord means submitting to him in all things, big and small. He is my Master. I do what he says. He asks that I place everything in my life under his command, that I make everything available to him. And, that means everything ... but everything. Including some things that I may be rather touchy about—like my money.

We surely know that citizenship in the Lord's kingdom calls from us, among other things, concrete support for his work. Out of the resources that he has blessed us with, some financial participation is in order. That would seem to go without saying. But, how much should we give? How much does he want?

God's Old Testament people had a very clear word from God about this. He asked for a very specific portion of all they possessed. *"Each year,"* Moses told the people, *"you shall tithe all the produce that grows in the field you have sown"* (Deut 14:22). In those days, money was not in such regular use as it is today. Barter was more common. Most of the people had only what their land produced or what they manufactured. So, they bartered, or traded, what they had in exchange for what they needed. The 'tithe' that Moses spoke of was to be given to support those who worked full-time for God and to take care of the expenses attached to the upkeep of their places of worship. And the tithe the Lord required of them was a full ten percent.

They had another very clear word from God in this matter as well. He promised to honour their faithfulness to the tithe. As they gave of their resources, he, in his turn, committed himself to making sure that their own needs were met. He promised that he would see to their being provided for. *"Give to the most high,"* the word of God states, *"as he has given to you, generously, and according to your means. For the Lord is one who always repays and will give back to you seven-fold"* (Sir 35:9-10). *"Bring the whole tithe into the storehouse, that there may be food in my house. And try me in this, says the Lord: shall I not open the floodgates of heaven to pour down blessings upon you without measure?"* (Mal 3:10).

It is worth noting that the Hebrew people to whom all this was addressed understood 'blessing' in a very material sense.

While we have no recorded words of Jesus in the matter of the tithe, neither do we hear him doing away with it. When he says: *"Give to Caesar what belongs to Caesar and to God what belongs to God"* (Matt 22:21), would his hearers not understand the tithe? That's what belongs to God, they would say.

He even restated the Lord's commitment to take care of those who were obedient to him. *"Stop worrying, then,"* he said, *"over what you are to eat, or what you are to drink, or what you are to wear. The non-believers are constantly running after these things. But, your heavenly Father already knows you need all these things. So, seek first the kingdom of God, therefore, and all these other things will be provided for you"* (Matt 6:31-33).

The earliest members of the Church went even further than the ten percent. *"Those who believed,"* Luke tells us, *"shared all things in common. They would sell their property and goods, dividing everything on the basis of each one's needs"* (Acts 2:44-45). This practice did not become universal in the Church, but it did serve as part of the inspiration for many of the religious communities that came later.

But what about us? What does the Lord expect today? Personally, I don't believe God's word on it has changed. Although I don't think he is placing it upon us as an obligation, I think he'd still like his tithe. And the tithe that he wants is ten percent—of my gross earnings, that is.

I can almost hear some saying: "That's gross! Ten percent! How am I supposed to pay my bills?" It is, for sure, a tough word. But I believe it's what God is saying.

And I believe, too, that his commitment to take care of his faithful ones still holds true as well. I've heard it again and again from people who have been tithing. They've never been, they say, as free from financial and temporal worries.

I heard it so often that I decided, some years ago, to try it myself. Although things were very tight for me financially at that time, I began to take ten percent off the top of my pay, such as it was, and give it to the Lord's work. I've been doing it ever since. And I've never been so well off. In fact, I'm being so well taken care of lately, I'm embarrassed.

But, for most of us, to begin tithing represents a rather radical shift in our priorities and perspectives. After I mentioned it at a meeting a while ago, one fellow reacted to the word by saying: "I've never heard of it before. I thought at first you meant teething." To which I thought an appropriate reply might have been: "If you think teething is painful, try tithing." Seriously, though, it's not at all painful. In fact, it works very well.

It almost, at times, seems more like an investment than anything else. This shouldn't be our motivation for getting into it, but the Lord just never fails to come through. I give to him and he gives to me. And it seems to work no matter how little or how much we earn. God is scrupulously faithful to his word. It's as simple as that.

I got an early lesson in generosity, and how the Lord blesses it, from the priest I mentioned in the previous chapter, a memory that I have recalled only in the last few years. He was quite simply the most generous person I have ever met.

He seemed continually to be giving things away. He gave away his money, his clothes, even, one day, his car. But he never wanted for anything. God provided. People were always giving things to him. It's hard to beat a deal like that.

Don't get me wrong. I'm not advocating we make a 'deal' with God. Nor do I recommend we approach the tithe with the notion of getting something out of it. I'm just plugging for something I believe God wants his people to do. To me, it's a matter of obedience, plain and simple.

If we decide to go for it, where should our money go? That, I think, is a matter between each person and God. Certainly, the body to which we belong, for most of us our parish, should come in for a good part of it. But, basically, we should consult him. We might tell him we'll send it wherever he says. In one way or other, he'll get through to us and make his will known.

For the neophyte, one who has never tithed, the full ten percent might represent too drastic a move to start with. Why not set a lower rate and gradually work up? But the important thing is to start.

Tithing will never make us rich. The Lord is not into that kind of thing, I don't think. But he is serious about taking care of his own.

Getting into the tithe means making a fairly radical response to the Gospel. But, I'm becoming convinced more and more that it's the radical stuff that works best. God likes it. He honours it. I know from experience it works. It works for him and his kingdom and it works for me.

If you're not already at it, why not take a deep breath and give it a try?

Handling Adversity

Sometimes it is necessary, even important, to state the obvious. Human life has its ups and downs. We are not very old before we are thrown into difficult situations and find we have to gather resources to cope or survive. What are we supposed to do when the resources wear thin? What is God's perspective on adversity? Does he have any directions about it for us?

First of all, the Lord wants us to know that he is not the cause of our trials. Whatever they are, there is another explanation as to where they come from. He does not cause poverty or sickness. He does not cause relationships to break down. He doesn't even cause death. The word of God says: *"God did not make death"* (Wis 1:13). Rather, all the evils that fall upon us are ultimately of our own making. God has offered us life, life in fullness. To enter into it, we have only to follow his way. Sadly, we have not always done this. We have chosen less than God at times, all of us. We have chosen less than life. That has, of necessity, meant death. Death has entered the world by man's choosing. All the other trials we encounter have the same basic cause. The cloud of sin that weighs upon human society is the root cause of all the adversity we experience.

However, God has offered us a reprieve. He has provided for us a Saviour, Jesus, his only-begotten Son. And Jesus has become for us the only way to the Father. *"I am the way, the truth, and the life,"* he said (John 14:6). In adversity of all kinds, then, our way out begins by turning to Jesus.

But, the trials will come. We can be well sure of that. We can get sick. We can have worries about job or money. Temptation is always a problem. Our hopes and expectations can be dashed.

We can become discouraged about our moral failures. Our relationships can fall apart. We can puzzle over what the Lord may be saying to us and feel we are getting it wrong again and again. Our reputations can be damaged. Stressful situations of all descriptions can confront us. We can feel unloved, be lonely. We can be misunderstood, our motives falsely judged. We can be pressed down by guilt. Our prayers can seem to go largely unanswered. We can fret over any manner of trial.

Does the Lord have any advice for us? St. Peter puts it this way: *"Do not be surprised, beloved, that a trial by fire is occurring in your midst ... Rejoice instead in the measure that you share in the sufferings of Christ. When his glory is revealed, you will rejoice in exultation"* (2 Pet 4:12-13). The author of the letter to the Hebrews says: *"Endure the trials that come upon you. Regard them as the discipline of God"* (Heb 12:7). St. James has another slant on it. *"Brothers,"* he says, *"count it pure joy when you are involved in every kind of trial. Realize that when your faith is tested, this makes for endurance"* (Jas 1:2-3). St. Paul says: *"All things work together unto good for those who love God"* (Rom 8:28). Saint Francis has his own special insights. He tells us that it is pure joy when we suffer every manner of rejection, especially when it comes from those whose call it is to love us in a particular way.

Can we see some of the things the Lord might want to teach us about adversity? He says he doesn't cause any of it, but he can use it all to mould us and to prepare us for what is to come. In any case, we are advised to rejoice when trials come because, in this way, we can be partakers in the sufferings of Jesus himself. We can even regard the difficulties of life as God's special training ground for those he loves. It is the Lord's boot camp. However burdensome the trials may be, the Lord wants us to know he has the capacity to set it right, to redeem it, and intends to do so.

Our adversity doesn't come from God. It comes from the badly messed up world we live in. More and more, the principles and values of our world are drifting from the Lord's way. As we stand up for the one in whom we believe and what he has taught us, we will find ourselves in more clearly direct opposition to the world around us. This can mean plenty of trouble. We can come in for all kinds of harassment. Because of man's fallen state, we are to expect it.

We can find some encouragement in the fact that Jesus himself, in taking upon himself our human nature, experienced adversity along with us. He, of course, took a strong, prophetic stand against the ways of the world, a world that had strayed far from the original plan of God. He was misunderstood. He was falsely judged. Opponents continually sought to discredit him. He was under an intense and constant pressure from the crowds of thousands who thronged to him with their problems and wounds. He was let down severely by those he was counting on, abandoned by most of them when he needed them most. And, finally, he was taken to the Cross, dying in suffering and shame, treated as the worst of criminals.

So, trials must come. What are we to do when they surface? Some suggestions are in order:

1. We must keep our focus upon the Lord and not upon the problem. We have to know that he understands our distress and means to sustain us through the difficulty.

2. We must offer it over to him. The Lord, though not the author of our ills, is able to use them to his purposes. As we turn them over to him, he is freed to make of them whatever he may deem appropriate. He will use them for our ultimate good.

3. We have to continue to give due praise and honour to God. Even thanksgiving. A good procedure to follow is to thank him for the blessings, the good things that happen, and to thank him in the things that happen that are not so good.

4. It is important for us, in each instance of adversity, to acknowledge whatever degree of sin or guilt may be ours. Sometimes, our problems are partly, or even totally, of our own making. We should simply repent, confess our sins, and let the Lord get on with his plan.

5. If someone else is involved in the difficulty, we should get it up front as quickly as possible, open it up with him or her, make it known to our spiritual director, our share group, or the community, whatever seems right. The Lord likes to operate in the light and not in the dark.

6. Whatever it is, we need to share it with others, at least one

other person, perhaps a brother who is very close. A difficulty shared is a difficulty cut in half.

7. We should ask the Lord for the strength, the grace, whatever we need to get through it. His help is available. He is close by and very interested.

8. We have to tell God we trust in him, that we intend to be faithful to him no matter what, and that we intend to persevere to the end.

In any case, we must respond to adversity in some way. We must do something about it. If we don't, we will have to resign ourselves to experiencing the results of stress. Our sleep patterns can get disturbed. We can feel knots in the stomach. We will find ourselves becoming overtired very easily, perhaps feeling tired most of the time. We might even begin to notice ourselves doing uncharacteristic things, giving into temper when things annoy us, saying and doing things that are downright silly.

Just as there are productive ways to cope with trials, positive things we can do to get things under control, so, likewise, there are things to avoid as we try to cope:

1. It is important, when a problem arises, not to look for someone else to blame.

2. We must not take it out on others when we ourselves are under strain. We have to avoid 'dumping' on those around us.

3. We have to avoid making excuses for whatever degree of fault may be ours.

4. We should avoid going silent and uncommunicative when things go wrong or we feel we have been offended. Sulking does not become us. We have to stay with the brothers and not go into withdrawal.

5. We have to be careful not to fall back into old, unre-

deemed patterns of behaviour, strategies that we habitually resorted to before we got serious about our relationship with the Lord. Things like throwing objects around, drinking, pornography, masturbation, developing and nursing grudges, disappearing into the television set, feverish activity, or a total entertainment mode.

Those are things to do and things not to do when adversity comes. But there are more remote things we can do to prepare ourselves for trial, patterns of action and attitudes which can serve to keep us in a state of readiness so that, when the inevitable hassles appear, we will be able to come through reasonably intact, and not succumb.

1. We must guard the entrance to our minds. We must be careful what we allow in.

2. We have to persevere with the ordered life. We have to stay with personal prayer and all the other disciplines the Lord has taught us.

3. We must protect our hearts by giving them daily to the Lord.

4. We have to stay in a continuing state of repentance.

5. It is vital that we forgive others whenever, and as soon as, we feel we have been offended. And we must get into the habit of asking forgiveness without delay of those whom we ourselves have offended.

6. We must use regularly the resources the Lord has provided for us. *"Put on the armour of God,"* St. Paul urges us, *"so that you may be able to stand firm against the tactics of the devil ... with the truth as the belt around your waist, justice as your breastplate ... zeal ... as your footgear ... faith ... as your shield ... the helmet of salvation and the sword of the spirit, the word of God"* (Eph 6:11-17).

7. We must frequent the Eucharist and the other sacraments

and make use of the sacramentals of the Church.

8. We have a special advocate through Jesus to the Father —Mary, our mother. We can ask her assistance.

9. We can ask the Lord to send angels to fight for us and watch over us.

Adversity, come though it must, is not meant to bring us down. The Lord will see us through if we are faithful to him. It has something to do with picking up the daily cross. Jesus reminds us: *"If any man wishes to become my disciple, he must take up his cross every day and follow along after me"* (Luke 9:23).

CHAPTER FOUR

Supporting One Another

The Lord's plan for the disciples of Jesus includes support structures for them. We are not meant, ordinarily, to live out our Christian commitment alone.

While relating closely to other people brings with it the potential for all manner of trial, the advantages are far greater. Anyone who has experienced genuine Christian community, whether it be parish-based or otherwise, will attest to God's presence in the midst of it.

But it isn't always easy. As in the case of everything worth striving for, we have to work at it. There are many feelings to deal with, many decisions to be made.

Loving One Another

If we are to be the Master's disciples, we must love one another. Jesus left no room for disagreement. In fact, our love for one another is to be the principal identifying characteristic of those who follow him. These are his words: *"By this will all men know that you are disciples of mine—if you have love for one another"* (John 13:35). If this is to be the case for all Christians, how much more so must it be true of those who form up one of the communities he has called into being?

We, the Companions of the Cross, have to take this injunction of the Lord very seriously and work at it. The love we speak of is not something that happens automatically. It is something that must be chosen by each of us.

Just what kind of love is Jesus talking about? How intense must be the love we have for one another? Here are more of his words: *"Love one another as I have loved you"* (John 13:34). How has he loved us? Hear him again: *"There is no greater love that a man can have than to lay down his life for his friends"* (John 15:13). He didn't, of course, just say it. He did it.

The love he wants us to share, then, is the kind that is deep enough, committed enough, persevering enough that, did the circumstances call for it, we would actually be willing to die for one another. It's a tall order. The Lord obviously wants us to be very involved with one another, developing a life together such that people will marvel at us, be so impressed by what they see that they will be convicted about who it is we follow. The love we share will draw people to Jesus himself.

It sounds good, doesn't it? Quite a challenge, but awfully good. But we have to move it out of the realm of theory into the realm of daily practice. Words are not enough. We have to live it. St. Paul has something to say about the kind of love we are to share. *"Make my joy complete,"* he urges the Christians, *"by your unanimity, possessing the one love, united in spirit and ideals. Never act out of rivalry or conceit. Rather, let all parties think humbly of others as superior to themselves, each of you looking to others' interests and not his own"* (Phil 2:2-4).

Do we all know that it is much easier to love everybody than it is to love the folks close by? It is easier to be a lover of mankind than to love those flesh and blood people with whom we rub shoulders every day. It isn't so easy to love them. It can, at times, be even difficult. It can be particularly difficult to love those who share my dwelling.

The members of my own household represent a special problem. I know them too well. Not only can I come to appreciate their finer qualities, those things that everybody outside the house can see readily enough, but I get into very close touch with their shortcomings too. When we live together, 24 hours a day, seven days a week, our faults and failings become awfully difficult to hide. We don't exactly want to let it all hang out, but it does anyway. It isn't easy to love people when their cruddiness faces us every day. But love them we must, warts and all.

It's amazing how little things can begin to loom so large when we live under the same roof. How do we feel about the one who talks so much, and invariably in a loud voice? Or who talks almost incessantly about himself? Or who doesn't talk at all? How about those who try to be funny a lot and just can't pull it off? The one who rattles his rosary? (Even St. Thérèse had trouble with that one.) What about the ones who never turn out the lights? Or who stay too long in the bathroom? And those whose interests are so categorically different from mine? It just isn't easy. And yet, these are the real live people the Lord wants me to love.

How can we do it? We have to make the choice. Love is a decision, a decision that God wants me to make. When I make it, he steps in and gives me the grace that renders it possible.

Love is total givenness. That's the way God loves—giving all and asking nothing back. I have to see love more as something I give than as something I receive. I have to say and do the loving thing continually without expecting it in return. If I can do that, it will work, because that's what love is, that's the way God himself loves. My love has to be given without counting the cost, has to be given with no strings attached. That's what God will bless. And that's what will make our love, make our life together, a ministry to others. They will see it and be drawn to the Lord himself.

Is it possible? It has to be. It's what the Lord is asking of us. He doesn't ask the impossible. It rests with us. We have to choose it. When we do, he will make it possible.

When we hear ourselves saying things like—"What about me? Why doesn't somebody do something for me for a change? What about my likes and dislikes?"—then we can be sure we are missing the boat. We are losing opportunities to love. Saint Francis said that love is at its best when we are getting nothing at all.

Love is a decision, a decision that God blesses. I still remember an experience I had several years ago. I was asked to give a day of renewal at Saranac Lake, New York. It comprised a couple of talks. I spoke about love and forgiveness, and how they are both primarily decisions and not feelings. When I was finished, a young woman came up to speak with me. She told me that she had listened carefully to what I had said, and was wondering if the Lord had meant the day's word very specifically for her. She explained her situation.

She was ten years married and had three children. But, as so often happens in this troubled day of ours, she and her spouse were having a rough time making a go of the marriage. She had no feelings left for him, she said. "In fact," she told me, "I can't stand the sight of him." She went on to explain that they were both now in the process of consulting lawyers and would be separating shortly. She didn't feel comfortable doing it, she said, in the light of her commitment to see it through for better or for worse, but there seemed to be no alternative. "But," she went on, "I heard what you said, and I am going to give it just one more chance. I'm going home, and I'm going to begin to say and to do the loving thing no matter how I feel. I don't know if I really believe that the Lord can do anything about it, but he's welcome to try." I left her, promising to keep her in prayer.

It was a year and a half later before I heard anything further. It came in the form of a letter. The testimony was very impressive. She had done precisely as she had said she would. She had begun to say and to do loving things despite her very negative feelings. "It wasn't easy," she said, "but I stuck with it." It worked. The relationship, after a while, began to heal. "Now," she wrote, "although I would not have thought it possible I could ever have said it again, I can truly say that I actually love the guy." She had made the Lord's decision, and he had gone to work to deal with her feelings.

The Lord's way works. He calls us to love one another, especially those who are closest to us, the ones who often are the most difficult to love. When we make the decision and do it, he blesses it.

Affirmation

The letter to the Hebrews says: *"Encourage one another daily"* (Heb 3:13). It seems the Lord has made us in such a way that we need to be told, on a fairly regular basis, that we're okay.

It goes almost without saying that those who are trying to live out their lives as brothers will have to get involved in bringing out the best in one another. Words of encouragement are in order. It is called affirmation.

I have to be convinced that those who are closest to me will love me for who I am, and not just for what I do. I have to know that, despite my mistakes, I am treasured. I must be sure that, my weaknesses notwithstanding, I have people around me who will stay around. When I mess up, I have to be confident that, after I confess my wrongdoing and resolve to make amends, all will be forgiven and forgotten. And even in the midst of my folly or transgression, I have to know that the love my brethren have for me will not grow cold, no matter what.

It's a rather tall order for a community. And yet, it is God's design. And it is something with which he will gift a body of brothers/sisters, provided each one will make the decision to love and to forgive one another.

This is a real need, not just a psychological conclusion. This is the way God has made us. We are meant to rely on one another. Brotherly support is not an option, especially for those who take on ministry within the Church. It is a necessity, a daily one at that.

The word of God is abundantly clear. *"Let us make it our aim ... to strengthen one another,"* St. Paul says (Rom 14:19). In fact, he says it again. *"With perfect humility, meekness, and patience, bear with one another lovingly"* (Eph 4:2). And again. *"Be kind to one another, compassionate, and mutually forgiving"* (Eph 4:32). And yet again. *"Comfort and upbuild one another"* (1 Thess 5:11).

If we are going to live out our lives as brothers in the Lord, we are going to have to seek out opportunities to affirm one another with sincerity and with regularity. Because we are participants in a wounded human nature, we tend to focus upon our own needs to such a degree that perhaps this is not so easy, not something that comes to us naturally. Just so, we will have, then, to make a conscious effort to do it. If we practise hard enough and persevere, we'll get good at it.

I don't have to wait until my brother does something good before I give some recognition to him, nor do I have to phrase my affirmation in elaborate words of praise. How about some simple things like: "It's just so good to have you around," or "You're a heck of a guy, you know," or "I hope you know you're a very special person." Wouldn't little words of encouragement like that not make others feel much better about themselves? Are some protesting that they'd feel awkward saying things like that? A little practice. That's all we need. We can all get good at it.

If I will concentrate more and more upon affirming my brothers, it will automatically take my focus off myself. That will be good for me. I will grow into greater maturity as a person and be deepening my own relationship with the Lord. The whole community will be a better place.

It is important for us to take positive steps to affirm our brothers. It is equally important that we avoid negative stuff. Negative humour has a subtly erosive effect on the good health of any community. It should be nipped in the bud.

We can so easily get to be experts at picking out the faults and weaknesses of our brothers and poking fun at them. But this will have a destructive effect on how they feel about themselves. We should never remind others of their past failures nor, in any way, go about trying to even the score. Differences between us have to be worked out in a more positive way.

Of course, affirmation can be overdone. There is no point in affirming a brother for his mistakes or foibles. Sometimes he will need to be called forth. But there is a way to do this. And we have to learn it.

We are all wounded to some degree. We might as well admit it. The healing we need can happen as we live together, respecting and supporting one another, loving one another as brothers. The better we all get at affirming one another, the more effective the healing process will be for all of us.

Unity

The Gospel writers report Jesus as praying a lot. He would get up early, find a 'lonely' place and be in communion with his Father (Mark 1:35). Included in his times of prayer were requests of all sorts. Among other things, he prayed all night before selecting the 12 apostles, presumably asking the Father's counsel about it.

My conviction is that his most fervent prayer was that his followers would be one, that they would be united heart and soul. *"I pray that they all may be one as you, Father, are in me, and I in you. I pray that they may be one in us so that the world may believe that you have sent me ... that their unity may be complete. It is by this that the world will know you have sent me"* (John 17:21-23). It is important, therefore, that we be one because God himself is one, and also because our unity will be the effective cause of people's coming to faith.

The Lord calls people together to share their lives with one another in him and so that he can use them to do his work. That's where the vision for any community comes from, from the overall plan of God to accomplish his purposes through bodies of disciples. It is their unity that God will use to make their work effective. It is their divisions that will bring the vision down.

Unity is God's doing. The Father, being perfectly one with the Son and the Holy Spirit, operates best through people who are one with him and one with one another. Because we tend so easily to divide one from another, the path to unity the Lord places us on will require a lot of purification, a lot of sandpapering. Strong and lasting unity among a body of disciples, among the members of a community, is hard to come by. Are some saying impossible? Not at all. Rare perhaps, but not impossible. Nothing is impossible with God (Mark 14:36). If God wants it, he can make it possible. It is for me to desire it with all my heart and to work for it with everything I've got.

Division, it is plain, is not God's work. We can readily see that. But can we see that is someone else's work? It is, for sure, the main tactic of our implacable foe, Satan. Ever since God began calling people together, urging them to be one, the enemy has been at work to divide them. It has, in fact, been his most successful enterprise. We live in a divided Church. Not only are there hundreds of different Christian denominations, there are serious divisions within our own Church. But, wherever the Lord can find a group of disciples who are willing to be one with one another, no matter how difficult it may be for them, he is ready to do powerful things.

As the Companions of the Cross, we have to be ready to sacrifice ourselves in the cause of unity. Whatever the cost, we have to be willing to pay it.

The unity the Lord wants from us is a unity of purpose. We feel we have a basic vision from the Lord for what we are to be. We are to be united around it. We can have differences of opinion about many things. We can have differences of style, different preferences. There is no problem with that. In fact, that's probably quite healthy. The unity we need will not be achieved by casting all of us into the same mould. We want to be one, but we don't need to be identical. We are not interested in cloning people. It is the vision, the Lord's word to us, we want to clone.

We can work for unity in many different ways. Here are a few practical steps we can all follow to facilitate the Lord's task of forging among us a oneness through which he can move:

1. I have to be eager to allow my brothers to be themselves. I have to give up my desire to see them conformed to patterns that I myself am most comfortable with.

2. I must be willing to work out the differences I am surely going to have with my brothers in the manner set down by the community. All of us must learn to dialogue our differences and to get help with the procedure when we need to.

3. I must find ways to serve my brothers and to affirm them.

4. I have to be ready to give up a lot of my own personal preferences in the interests of developing that greater life that we are to have in common.

5. At all costs, I must avoid gossip, idle talk about absent brothers.

6. I must pray daily for my brothers, mentioning each one by name before the Lord.

7. I must desire to have close unity with my brothers and work for it with all my heart as the Lord directs.

We don't have to be identical in all things. The Father, the Son, and the Holy Spirit are very one, but they are not identical. Each has his own role. We don't have to be identical, but we do have to be united.

How united are we to be? Jesus has said that we are to be one just as he is one with his Father. How one is that? One day, the apostle Philip asked Jesus to let the disciples see the Father, just once. One look at the Father and we'll be satisfied, he said. Jesus' response? "Philip," he said, "you have been with me all this time and you can make a request like that? Philip, if you have seen me, you have already seen the Father" (John 14:9). Now, that's really one. That's a lot of unity. But, Jesus urges it of us. Are we willing to go for it?

Reconciling With One Another
The Gospel's word on loving one another and being one with one another is just too plain to deny. *"Love one another as I have loved you,"* Jesus tells his disciples (John 13:34). *"Make every effort to preserve the unity which has the Spirit as its origin and peace as its binding force,"* St. Paul writes (Eph 4:3).

Unfortunately, because we're human, we offend one another. We fall out with our brothers and sisters. We are not in relationship very long with others before we need to be asking for their forgiveness. We have a regularly recurring need for reconciliation. It is important for us to know how to go about it. We must develop a heart for it. We must desire with a real longing to maintain the unity the Lord wants us to have. This is not always easy. If someone has offended me, I may not feel much like getting it straightened out with him. It is a lot easier just to nurture a grudge. If we don't have the heart for it, we might try asking God to grant it.

There is a lot of potential for effective reconciliation in a group of committed people like the Companions of the Cross. I can safely assume that all the brothers are of good heart, that they are sincere and as concerned about the kingdom of God as I am.

It will require that I get practical about getting the necessary reconciliation underway. If I sense the need for it, rather than wait for my brother to do it, I should take the initiative myself. We'll have to set a time and place for us to meet, just the two of us.

It goes without saying that we should get the conversation started with a short prayer. It will probably work best if we try to deal with one item at a time. It will facilitate things if only one tries to talk at a time and if neither interrupts the other when he's speaking. Our vocabulary should be free of confrontational or judgmental terms, such as 'silly' or 'unreasonable'.

We have to be careful how we say things. Rather than begin by saying: "You said ...", it would be better to phrase it something like: "I thought I heard you say ..." At the same time, it is important for us to be quite honest. If I have been hurt by something said or done, I have to say so. I might try it, however, in a nonthreatening way, like: "You probably meant nothing by it, but I was really hurt when you ..."

We have to remember that our meeting is a dialogue. There is no point in my trying to gain the upper hand. It isn't a contest. There isn't to be a winner and a loser. As a matter of fact, we are both meant to be winners. I am not to be interested in proving myself right. That is of no importance at all. I have to keep in mind that the purpose of dialogue is to understand the brother's point of view, to gain an appreciation of where he's coming from. It is not important to find out who is to blame. We are not meeting to lay guilt trips on each other.

Accusations are out of place. Words like: "You're not perfect either, you know," or "Don't you talk," or "Yes, but you said ..." have no place in a reconciliation session. If they occur, we'll only need more reconciling later. We must also avoid making judgments. An observation is one thing. No harm in that. But judgment is another thing. Lots of harm in that. If I say: "You have been going 14 to 16 hours a day for the past week," I'm not (provided it's true) out of line. But, If I add: "What are you trying to do—save the world?" then I am way out of line. Jesus speaks a word about that. *"Judge not, lest you yourself be judged,"* he says (Luke 6:37).

If, as the dialogue goes on, I become convicted that I have actually wronged my brother, even in a small way, or even inadvertently, I should say I'm sorry and ask him for forgiveness. If he asks forgiveness of me, I have no choice: I must forgive. It doesn't depend on my feelings. Some say they can't forgive because they don't feel it. Not so. Forgiveness is not a feeling. It is a decision. It's like trusting God or getting up in the morning. The Lord wants both of these no matter how we feel. And he wants forgiveness in the same way. After all, the Lord has forgiven us. And we probably haven't deserved it either.

It is important to get all items aired. Even if we need a second meeting, it is vital to complete the process. It may be painful, but it's worth it. We have to persevere to the end.

If our dialogue reaches an impasse, we should invite the assistance of a third brother, one who is not likely to take sides.

The reconciliation, when finished, has to be lived out. We have to be able to become friends and talk again, even to spend time together. In a very real way, it is true that, if we can't play together, it is quite unlikely that we will be able to pray together.

Jesus puts it in a way that leaves no room for alternatives. He says: *"If you come before the altar to offer your gift to God and there you remember that your brother has something against you, go first and be reconciled with your brother. Then come and offer your gift"* (Matt 5:23-24).

The community, the Companions of the Cross, considers this whole matter of prime importance, so important that we have placed ourselves under obedience to work out our grievances in this way, to enter into dialogue and to become reconciled. We believe that, if we don't, we're stuck. We believe the Lord is completely unwilling to accomplish his full purposes with us unless we love, and are one with, one another. That means being reconciled.

CHAPTER FIVE

Companions of the Cross

Background

The community traces its roots to a small share group of four men which began to meet on a weekly basis in January of 1984. It comprised a priest, a seminarian, and two others who were preparing to enter the seminary in September of that year. It was only a mutual support group. Nothing further was foreseen. A fifth man was added in September as he, too, began seminary studies.

Over the course of the next year, as the members remained faithful to their weekly gatherings and pursued the Lord's word, a sense began to develop that the Lord had additional plans.

By May, 1985, the vision as outlined below was substantially in place. And it was as though the Lord was saying something like: "If you will accept the call I am giving you, remain faithful to me and to one another, I will bring others in and quickly add to your number."

As of this date, September 15, 1989, the community numbers seven priests and 18 other men who are pursuing studies for the priesthood.

A Short History

The Companions of the Cross trace their beginnings to a small share group that started weekly meetings in January of 1984. It was made up of a priest, a seminarian and two younger men who were to enter the seminary the following September. It was to function as a supplementary support group for the seminarians during their years of study. Nothing further was foreseen.

The meetings comprised a short time of communal and spontaneous praise, a time of listening to the Lord, a time of sharing the victories and struggles of the previous week, and a time of ministry (prayer for each one's needs). The original venue was the Catholic Renewal Centre on the campus of St. Pius X High School in Ottawa. When Fr. Bob Bedard, the priest involved, was appointed to St. Mary's Church in November of '84, the meetings moved there.

It is interesting to note that, two days before Fr. Bob's appointment to St. Mary's, one of the young men reported an image in which the pastor-in-waiting was standing on a box surrounded by little clown figures. A church came into focus not too far distant, and, when Father pointed it out and beckoned to them, all the clowns followed him into the church.

When the archbishop asked Fr. Bob to take on the pastorate at St. Mary's, he said (because of the coincidences that surrounded the appointment): "I have seen the finger of God. The Holy Spirit wants you to go to St. Mary's."

In late 1984, the members of the share group received what they believed was an authentic word from the Lord, what they have come since to regard as the first of their three pivotal words, words that began to point them in the direction of community. The implications were in no way clear to them, but they sensed the Lord was saying to them that the relationships that were now building were to endure beyond ordination. Thus, the group was not just a support structure for the seminary years, but something more. They began to respond to the word by beginning to refer to one another as "the brothers."

It is important to understand how it is possible for God to convey his intentions to a group of people. If they are seeking his word, determined to carry it out whatever it is, and waiting patiently for him, he will often communicate his intention to one of the people involved. When this person brings the possible word to the group for discernment, and each of the others affirms it quickly, there can be a good degree of assurance the word is from God. Of course, it doesn't always work this way. There can be degrees of certainty. The discernment process is often longer and more involved, but it's nice, once in a while, to be able to catch it without a delay.

In the beginning, this is how it worked with 'the brothers.' The word was spoken into the meeting and confirmed immediately by the others. It still works that way at times.

The members of the share group began then to have the sense that they were to seek the Lord's word for them as a group. They felt that God was saying that he had plans for them, that they should accept a ministry from Mary and be placed under her protective mantle, and that the implications of where they were headed were largely hidden from their view.

The second of the three pivotal words was received several weeks into 1985. One of the members said one night (by this time the meetings had moved to Friday evenings) that he believed the Lord wanted the brothers to work together. Immediately, all the others confirmed the word. The Lord seemed to be saying that he had a "new work" for them to do, that he was beginning "a bold new action," and that they should direct their energy to "building a strong brotherhood" among themselves. They felt they were soon being directed to find "creative ways to be and to work together."

All this resonated strongly within their spirits. But, while they had firm convictions about it, they had to confess to being quite puzzled as to how they might be real brothers and effectively work together. The nature of the diocesan priesthood is that men are appointed to different points of the diocese and get involved in very full agendas, leaving relatively little time to explore common ministry or build deep and lasting relationships. Much discussion followed as the meetings continued and resolutions were taken to be faithful to the Lord's word in whatever ways would seem appropriate or possible.

Around Easter of 1985, the third and final pivotal or directional word was received. One of the men said something like the following: "I don't know how the rest of you will react to this. It seems a bit far out, but I really feel the Lord wants these brothers to live together." As radical as the word was, all the others confirmed it at once. The principal implication dawned upon them at once. God wanted a new community of priests, a canonical body to which he could give specific ministry directions.

Not too long afterwards, a word was spoken into the meeting that has had considerable teaching value for the community ever since. The Lord seemed to be saying: "I want you to become skilled at waiting for me." Waiting was to be understood as a skill and not as a gift. We had to decide to do it, and eventually get good at it. This has served the community well. The Lord has been making clear to the brothers that they need his sense of timing. He has been showing them that there can be a waiting period between the giving of a vision or a direction and the time for its actualization. The example of St. Paul has been meaningful. The waiting time between his powerful experience on the road to Damascus (Acts 9), the very explicit word that he was to be used to bring the Gospel to the Greek world, and his actual call to Antioch by Barnabas (Acts 13) when this ministry began, was a minimum of eight years. The brothers settled in to do some serious waiting.

The vision for the community began to come quickly then. The brothers were to be a body that would live under the total Lordship of Jesus, promote devotion to the Eucharist, use all the ministry gifts of the Holy Spirit, be consecrated to Jesus through the Immaculate Heart of Mary, be loyal to the Pope and the Magisterium of the Church, embrace a simple lifestyle, and minister to the poor.

The Lord seemed to be saying to the brothers that, if they would embrace the ministry vision, he would add to their number significantly and quickly. This seemed quite unlikely since it had taken a year and a half for the membership to grow from four to five. Nonetheless, within a few months, over 15 men were meeting on Friday nights. It struck the brothers that they themselves had not recruited any of the newcomers. They thus quickly came to the conclusion that the Lord himself was to be the vocations director, and to this day they have not advertised their existence outside their own modest newsletter.

The remainder of 1985 was characterized by three other noteworthy events. First, John Vandenakker, the original seminarian, became the first of the brothers to be ordained (June) to the priesthood. Second, one of the men reported an image (October) he had received in prayer that had Jesus presenting each of the brothers with a cross. Although they didn't realize it at the time, this had to do with the name the community would receive. And third, Archbishop Plourde gave preliminary approval (November) to the community's existence saying that he himself had had a similar vision for the priesthood of the future. The brothers thus began their canonical existence as an informal association (Canon 299) within the Church. They were on their way.

A cautionary word got 1986 started. The brothers were reminded that nothing worthwhile for the Lord could be built without some cost. When the Lord goes to work, they were told, the enemy gets nervous and begins to play upon the weaknesses of people. The group was to experience a bit of harassment, something like the master they were pledged to follow. The year was not too far along before the brothers began to carry labels of all sorts. "It's a cult," some charged. Another even said, "There are evil spirits at work here!" They were called conservative (because of their theology) on the one hand, and liberal (because of their style of worship) on the other. "They're divisive," was a common assessment. One summed it up by saying, "We don't need this kind of thing in Ottawa."

Through it all, the men had the sense the Lord was calling them to remain calm, embrace the Cross, and trust in him. They seemed to hear him say that it was his enterprise and that he would steer it where he wanted it to go.

The conviction began to deepen among the members that the community was not to be an Ottawa phenomenon, nor even largely Canadian, but that, rather, they were to expect it to develop along international lines and to expect, fairly early, a good bit of American participation.

One day, in early autumn, the community received its name. It was during Sunday high Mass that Fr. Bob's homily included the phrase "companions of the Cross." Although he did not use it with any reference to the community, several brothers in attendance that day said to themselves: "That's it! That's our name!" It was quickly discerned that this was what the Lord would have the community called. It was September 14, the feast of the Exultation of the Holy Cross.

In October of that year, the second of the brothers was ordained to the priesthood. Originally a student for the Diocese of Hamilton, Dennis Hayes had decided, at the conclusion of his theological studies, to postpone ordination due to a gnawing sense that the Lord had something different in mind for him. Led to Ottawa in the spring of '85, he connected with the brothers. Before long, he felt sure this was his call.

Shortly after Dennis' ordination, one of the priests of the Archdiocese of Ottawa, the community's home base, Fr. Jim Whalen, indicated interest in joining the community. The brothers felt this was possible confirmation of a previous word that had suggested priests, already ordained, would join them.

Archbishop Plourde had said more than once that the charism of the community would come clear as we, in union with him, would persevere in consulting the Holy Spirit. At a meeting with Fr. Bob in Holy Week, 1987, he said: "I have a dream for your community. It must not be conservationist. It is to be evangelistic. I would like you to take on three main apostolates—the poor, alienated Catholics, and youth." When a bishop speaks like that, his word becomes the word of God for those for whom it is intended. The Companions of the Cross very quickly confirmed the word and became determined to point to the day when they could begin serious efforts to take up the ministries the Archbishop was indicating.

That summer, the brothers sensed the time had come to prepare their statutes and petition for official canonical status within the Church. Father Bob and Rick Jaworski, one of the brothers, set to work to put them together. They were submitted to the Archbishop for approval in September of 1987. After his suggestions for revision were included, they were eventually approved and officially promulgated February 11, 1988, the feast of Our Lady of Lourdes.

The Companions of the Cross thus became a public association of clerics as defined in canons 312-320. A few years down the road, when the Lord indicates his time has come, they will apply for status as a 'society of apostolic life' according to canons 731-746, a status that will give them control over the formation of the candidates and over the appointments of the priests.

The community received some additional good news when J. David Bernard, a brother who had gone to the Diocese of St. Paul in Alberta seeking ordination, reported that his date for priesthood had been set for August 15. This was a remarkable fulfillment of a sense that he had had the previous fall, when it appeared he might not be ordained at all, that he would be a priest before the Marian Year was out. The date of his ordination, August 15, 1988, the feast of the Assumption of the Blessed Virgin Mary, was the final day of the Marian Year.

The brothers, having been, they believed, called by the Lord to become a community of priests and to live together, and having now received official status within the Church as a public association, were wondering when the Lord would arrange it so that they could actually begin to live out their vision for shared life and shared ministry. They had learned by this time, however, to do a lot of praying and a lot of waiting upon God. They were making no moves to try to force open any doors. But, unexpectedly, in June of 1988, Archbishop Plourde appointed Fr. John to join Fr. Bob at St. Mary's. His further word was that the others would be permitted to take up common residence a year from that time. As to common ministry beyond that, he said they would have to wait (a concept the brothers were getting used to) until ongoing developments in the diocese would make it possible.

Since September, 1986, the brothers had been meeting with lay people who had gathered around to support the development of the vision. In order to make it more possible for the brothers to develop the direction the Lord was giving them, they began in September of 1988, to hold their weekly meeting separately from the gatherings of their lay associates. They moved the Friday evening get-together across town to St. Margaret Mary's parish hall. It was thought that this move would assist both groups to move ahead according to the Lord's plan.

A number of additional words began to take root in the heart of the community as the fall season got underway. They felt the Lord was telling them that they would be "overtaken by events that you will be required simply to react to. These will overtake you, not overcome you. Keep your gaze upon me and not on the events. I am in charge. Do not fear." They were cautioned that they would experience an intensifying of the spiritual battle to which all who strive to follow the Lord unreservedly can attest. But God seemed to be calling them to do a bit of "trail-blazing" in the whole area of the renewal of the diocesan priesthood. They were to hang in there with him no matter what was to happen. He would see them through.

The vision for the lay association finally became clear and was articulated in May of 1989.

The brothers, the associates, and a host of family and friends gathered together in joy and gratitude to celebrate their fourth ordination in June of the same year. Roger Vandenakker saw his call to the priesthood confirmed and actualized by the laying on of the Archbishop's hands.

At the time of this writing, the brothers feel that they are in a phase of consolidation. They are to stay together, trusting in the Lord, making every possible effort to forge the unity upon which he can build, embracing the daily cross faithfully, and keeping their eyes firmly upon him.

They do not have any grandiose or exalted plans. They are content to be but a very small chip in the overall mosaic God himself is designing in this age to work a powerful revival in his Church.

The Priesthood

We are speaking about the priesthood of Jesus Christ, *"the eternal high priest"* (Heb 6:20). If there is concern about defining the role of the priest within the Church today, we have simply to look to Jesus himself. A priest will do whatever Jesus did.

Jesus was a Father to his flock. He made visible on earth for them and for us the Fatherhood of God. He shepherded them. A priest must do the same.

We need to see the priest as the father-substitute that God appoints for his family on earth.

It is not easy to be a father today. The great masses of physically and emotionally absent fathers have served to produce a largely unfathered people.

Men in general are not in good shape. Keeping in mind the many delightful exceptions that there certainly are, we could probably make a rather good case for a crisis in masculinity in our time. Males, the statistics tell us, account for 75% of all suicides, 88% of all arrests for drunk driving, and are subjects of six out of seven drug-related charges. We don't have any really accurate numbers, but the percentage of men among those who are active in the Church is much lower than it needs to be.

Into this constituency of God's people who are, to a great extent, either inadequately fathered or not fathered at all, steps the priest. It will not be easy for him to father these people. And yet, that is what he must do. He must do what Jesus did.

Everything else that the priest is to do must flow from his role as father to God's flock. He will preside over family occasions, liturgical or otherwise. He will affirm his people, calling them, as any good father must do, into their true identities as sons and daughters of God. He will bless and anoint them. He will represent them before the throne of God, standing as a mediator and pleading their cause. He will seek the direction of God himself, his wisdom, for his people. He will then proclaim the word of the Lord and call others to embrace it and live it out. He will call people to specific ministries within the Body of Christ, prepare them to fulfill the tasks, mandate them in the name of the Lord, and send them out to serve God's purposes. He will encourage them, support them, be a steadying influence for them, be their rallying point. He will call them forth when they step out of line, correct them, absolve them, and heal their wounds. He will rejoice with them in their good times and grieve with them in their sorrows.

All these things Jesus did. All these things a father must do. This is the priest's own mandate, his agenda.

His job will also include catching the Lord's vision for his people. He will need all the input they can give him and he will have to spend lots of time trying to receive the Lord's word in prayer.

He will involve himself in the Church's principal mission, the proclamation of God's good news of life in Christ, and take the lead preaching in season and out, calling all who will listen to turn their lives over to the Lord. He will, in his own person, represent God's people everywhere he goes.

It is very easy for a priest to get caught up with other things. He must resist the temptation. When the apostles found that their attention was being more and more taken up with other things, they moved quickly to a solution. They delegated others to the daily tasks so that they could concentrate upon *"prayer and the service of the word"* (Acts 6:4), so that they could, in short, shepherd the Lord's flock. They were not to be tyrannized by the urgent, as so many of us priests tend to be today.

In order for the Lord's family, the Church, to function according to his plan, the priest, first of all, must fulfill the role designated for him. He must have a clear notion of who and what he is to be. But he must not take over the tasks that the Lord has in mind for others. Just as a father is not meant to co-opt all family functions, neither must the priest. In fact, the Church, at any level, does not accomplish what it is supposed to, according to the plan of God, when the priest over-functions, when he usurps the roles of others. Just as it is clear what the priest is to be and to do, so it is likewise clear what he is to leave to others.

He is not to be an administrator. It is probably best if somebody else knows where the keys are, adds up the columns of figures, deals with the bank, calls the plumber, buys the food, writes the cheques, locks and unlocks the church, and turns off the lights. The priest is not a details man. Let him immerse himself in prayer and God's word and beg the Lord for his vision and direction.

The priest is not a counsellor. He is not the answer to everybody's problem. In my experience, the great majority of people who are convinced they 'have to speak to a priest' don't really have to at all. They may certainly need to talk, but my conviction is that other people will have more gifts from God in the area of counselling than will priests. Part of the priest's own charism will be to identify the gifts in others, to call them forth, to prepare them for ministry, to send them forth, and to support them.

He is not an organizer. It is better if he doesn't put the parish picnics or pot-luck suppers together. And hopefully he will find that other people are much better at conducting meetings and more efficient at setting up parish council elections.

The priest is not a sacristan, a porter, an office manager, a decorator. It is not that these tasks are below him. It is just that they are not his tasks.

When we get right down to it, most of the Church's ministries are proper, not to the priest at all, but to lay people. They can counsel, organize, administer, teach, prepare children for the sacraments, instruct adults in the faith, conduct marriage preparation programs, run meetings, decorate the church, plan the liturgies, lead the music, conduct devotions (Rosary, Stations of the Cross) and para-liturgical services, visit the sick (bring them Holy Communion, too), visit the lonely, the elderly, and those in prison, feed the hungry, house the homeless, rescue the abandoned, take up the Church's great causes of life, justice, and peace, minister to young people of all ages, minister to families in trouble, form prayer teams for intercession and inner healing. The list could go on and on.

The family of God is out of order and doesn't function according to his plan when the priest tries to involve himself in doing things that other people are called to do. But let's not be too quick to fault him. After all, he is the man on the spot, the one with the highest profile among God's people, the one who most often finds himself in the eye of the storm. It is understandable, I guess, considering the experience we have had, for people to turn to him for everything and to expect he will have all the answers. It is so easy for him to be captured by the immediate need. But if he allows himself to be drawn into things he should stay out of, he will either neglect the work (prayer and service of the word) he's supposed to do or he will burn out trying to do everything.

Speaking only for myself, I'd have to say that the preparation I received years ago for my role as a priest among God's people, did not get me ready very well at all for what I see now I am supposed to do. I think most of my contemporaries would agree. We were not trained to work with teams of lay people, people who would do sensitive ministry with us. Rather, we understood that we were to do our best to meet whatever needs people might have. We were to involve ourselves in continual crisis response. Ours was to be a ministry of availability.

I believe we have to be faithful to Vatican II, rethink all of that, and begin to see it very differently. I am convinced our priority as priests must be to see what God is doing and to minister to that. This may well be a time of God's special visitation. There are many indications that he is releasing the power of his Holy Spirit in greater and greater measure. He is on the move. He is doing the initiating. We have to recognize his initiatives, point them out to our people, and seek the Lord as to how best we are to react. If we let him, he will do the acting. It will be for us to do the reacting.

But the priest is, in any case, to be a blessing to his people. God can do wondrous things through those whom he appoints as heads over the many segments of his family. He has said so himself. *"I will lavish choice portions upon the priests, and my people shall be filled with my blessings"* (Jer 31:14).

The life of a priest is not always an easy one. But there is truly nothing quite like it. There's nothing like watching God go to work. As priests, we are privileged to be right on the front line, involved in the thick of the action. If I had it to do all over again, I'd do exactly the same thing. I'd become a priest.

Are there young (or not so young) men out there considering a possible call to the priesthood today? Let them consider it well. It's an exciting time to be a priest. The Lord is doing something very special in our day. He has initiated a thoroughgoing renewal of the whole Church. And he is calling men from the four corners of the Church into the priesthood, men whom he will train to lead the way. Anyone whom the Lord may be tapping on the shoulder would do well not to miss it.

Jesus related to his disciples as a father to his family. A priest must do the same. It is not to be wondered at, I guess, if everybody calls him 'Father'.

Celibacy

Jesus said a curious thing one day. In the context of a teaching he was giving on marriage, he introduced a notion that was quite new. He put it this way: *"Some are eunuchs from birth. Others are eunuchs of the court. Still others are eunuchs for the sake of the kingdom. Let those who can accept it embrace it"* (Matt 19:12). He obviously had something in mind.

He was clearly telling them and us that celibacy is both a call from God and a gift to the Church. He was saying that it could be instrumental in accomplishing God's purposes on earth, useful for the building up of the kingdom.

Celibacy, Jesus has taught us, is an invitation from God, not a command. If those who are called by the Lord will say 'yes', he will give them the gift to live it out.

How many are called to this by God? We cannot know for sure, but it is my own conviction that there are probably a great many more called than are accepting the invitation.

Celibacy, of course, does not get a very high rating in the world's eyes. In fact, it's probably looked upon as strange by many. At best, it is little understood. The secular mind simply cannot grasp the concept. Opinions about celibates would range from: "I think they must have some kind of hormonal deficiency," to "They must have something going on the side." Assessments of this kind do not, obviously, make it any easier for those hearing the call to give it any serious consideration.

The world has its point of view. On everything. What we

have to do, in all things, is try to get hold of God's point of view. What are his purposes for calling people to celibacy? How does he see it? How, in his eyes, is it possible, or even life-giving, for us?

I believe the Lord wants us to know that celibacy is not to be defined in negative terms. It is not just a matter of abstaining from sexual activity. Rather, it is a foregoing of love and intimacy with one person in order to make it possible for us to love and have intimate relationships with many. The former, of course, includes sexual sharing, and the latter does not. God calls some to be his partners in loving others. He issues an invitation to belong uniquely to him and to his people, the Church.

Celibacy is, of course, a prophetic statement both to the Church and to the world. It points to mankind's ultimate destiny. *"When people rise from the dead,"* Jesus teaches us, *"they neither marry nor are given in marriage. They live in heaven like the angels"* (Matt 22:30).

The whole thing is based upon the reality that total human fulfillment and completion are available from God. *"O Lord, you are my portion and my cup"* (Ps 16:5), the psalmist writes.

Saint Paul's position on the matter is on plain record. *"The unmarried man,"* he writes, *"can be busy with the Lord's affairs, concerned about pleasing the Lord. But the married man has to be busy with the world's demands because he must please his wife"* (1 Cor 7:32-33).

What is to be said to those who sense the Lord may be offering them this way of helping build up the kingdom? How is it to be possible for them to live out this call? Jesus has the answer. Let them accept it. What God calls for, he makes possible. Not only that, he makes it rewarding and growth-producing for anyone so called. It is not meant to be a titanic struggle. It is meant to be an experience of the ongoing grace of God. It is not intended to be made possible by cold showers and rigorous discipline, but by the always more-than-sufficient power of God.

Some, well schooled in the academic disciplines of the world, would object: "But, surely, all normal human beings need sex." Not so. It is not a need. A desire, to be sure, a drive, an urge. But, with all due respect to the behavioural sciences, not a need. It is not a need in the same sense as food or sleep. By the design of God himself, we are drawn to sexual fulfillment. We are enticed in its direction. And with good reason. It has an obvious connection with God's plan for the continuation of the human race. But, by God's call, some, perhaps many, of us are invited to hear a different word.

Is it not necessarily a lonely type of life, many will ask? Not at all. Loneliness is the incapacity to share one's feelings. We can be lonely in the midst of a crowd. We can be lonely in marriage. The celibate person has perhaps even more potential for many close relationships than does the one who is married, more opportunity to share the victories and struggles of life.

There is an evident connection within the greater part of the Catholic Church between celibacy and the priesthood. Why does the discipline of the Church require priests to be celibate? It is a matter of order, of course, and not doctrine, and could change.

But there is probably a lot of wisdom in the discipline. The priest is to act in the person of Christ himself, to do the things he did, to be what he was. Jesus remained celibate.

Celibacy is both a call from God and a gift from him. Those of us who have accepted the call must learn to count on the Lord to come through with the gift. But, like all of God's gifts, we must ask for it. If we have made the choice to accept it, stay faithfully with that decision, and ask regularly for the gift, the Lord will give it.

God knows that we all need intimacy, affirmation, close personal relationships, fulfillment, identity, security. He can supply all these things to us whether we are married or not, whether we are celibate or not. What is important is: what is he calling for from me?

The Cross

We are the Companions of the Cross. We have to know we did not come upon our name by accident. We believe it's what the Lord wants us called. We are happy to carry such an identity. The implications in the title, however, present a challenge.

The Cross is the instrument of our salvation. Without it, the gates to life would have remained closed. Mankind's sin, our rebellion against God, cut us off from him permanently. Atonement was our only hope. Only the blood of Jesus, shed in reparation, was good enough.

We have been redeemed, thanks be to God. But the price was exceedingly high. The cost was enormous. It took the agony and death of the divine Son of God himself.

But it's been done. Eternal life is now possible for every human being. However, each one has to choose it. We have, each of us, to repent of our own sins and believe that Jesus is the authentic one, the one sent from the Father. And this takes an additional grace, a grace that God alone can give. He will give it in response to prayer, to fasting, to penance, and to good works. This is why St. Paul urges us, putting it in an unusual way, to make up what is lacking in the sufferings of Christ (Col 1:24).

This is called carrying the daily cross. It is an essential mark of the true disciple. *"Unless you take up your cross every day,"* Jesus said, *"and carry it after me, you cannot be my disciple"* (Luke 9:23).

We join our sufferings to his. We take our burdens, our anxieties, our pain, our misery, our disappointments, and we join them to his. We carry our daily cross.

It requires a kind of death from us. But this death can be productive. Is that what Jesus meant when he talked about the grain of wheat? *"You see this grain of wheat?"* he asked. *"Unless it fall to the ground and die, it remains only a grain of wheat. But, if it does die, it will produce much fruit"* (John 12:24). And he went on to say: *"Whoever loves his life will lose it, but whoever hates his life in this world, will preserve it unto life eternal"* (John 12:25).

It is all imitative of God, and it has to do with love. God is love itself (1 John 4:16). He loves totally. The Father and the Son so love each other, with a love of total givenness, that the love between them is, eternally, another person, a person Jesus has taught us to call the Holy Spirit. God loves without any strings attached. There is nothing we can do to make him love us any more than he does. And there is nothing we can do to make him love us any less. He loves without asking anything back. It is a kind of dying. To the extent that we can imitate that kind of love, our love will be very fruitful.

God took a great risk in creating us the way he did. He wants us to share his life, to live with him, to take prepared seats around his table—and forever. But in order for us to qualify, we have to be free. We have to freely choose to love God. It means, of course, that we can freely choose not to love him. An unrequited love is extremely painful. That's the risk he's taken. But that's the way love is: it takes risks.

This is something the world has a lot of trouble with. A God who is total risk, total giving, total abandonment—this is hard to handle. It goes against all the world's common sense. To look at Jesus on the Cross—helpless, weak, broken, nailed, wounded, despised, rejected, vanquished, a dying God—forces a confrontation within us. The Cross just doesn't make sense.

Saint Paul called it God's folly, his foolish love. It was madness to the Gentiles, a stumbling block to the Jews (1 Cor 18-25). The Cross is the sign of contradiction.

The message of the Cross is at odds with our nature, our fallen nature. So much of what is natural is just not good —revenge, theft, lust, hatred, grudges. Salvation through the Cross means being lifted up above the natural to something higher, to share the very life of God. And he means it to begin now for us and never to end.

Picking up the daily cross means loving foolishly, loving the way God loves. It means joining in with his folly. It demands a rejection of the world's ways, the best of worldly wisdom, things like—'do your own thing', 'have your own way', 'be your own boss', 'be good to yourself', 'be secure', 'don't get involved'. It means the surrendering of the human intellect, the faculty of which we are so proud, admitting we don't have all the answers. It involves the giving over of the human will and choosing only what God wants. It brings us to put an end in our lives of the game of control.

Jesus calls us to embrace the Cross. He doesn't suggest that we should like it. Our human nature will cry out in protest. We are not to feel guilty about this. We are partakers in a fallen human nature. That's what's in the process of being redeemed. As we choose to pick up our cross and follow Jesus, we will be getting purified. God is not finished with us yet.

The Cross means bringing my will into line with the will of the Father. That's what Jesus did. *"My food,"* he said, *"is to do the will of the one who sent me"* (John 4:34). Sometimes it can be very painful. Jesus persevered, nonetheless, right to the end. *"Father,"* he had prayed, *"if it be possible, let this cup pass me by. But not as I will. Your will be done"* (Mark 14:36).

We, the Companions of the Cross, find ourselves caught up in this folly. We have been tantalized by Jesus. We have been fascinated by him, dazzled. We have been trapped and captured. We are prisoners of the Lord. But we are delighted to be in his custody. We would not want it any other way. We are able to say with St. Paul that we have reappraised all else as rubbish in the light of knowing Christ Jesus, that we are now racing to capture the prize for which he has captured us (Phil 3:12).

The Companions of the Cross want to be faithful to the Lord's call. It involves embracing the cross we find each day. If it's heavy, it means embracing it anyway. We will have to do more than wear the Cross. We will have to carry it.

Basic Components of the Vision

When we felt the Lord indicating to us that he wanted a new community, it was our impression that, if we agreed to launch out into the unknown as the whole thing seemed to imply, God would quickly lay out the basic vision for us. Following are the seven main planks in the platform we thought the Lord wanted us to stand on.

1. Jesus is Lord
As St. Paul has said: *"The Father has made him Lord of all."* The earliest Christians summarized their beliefs and greeted one another with the words: "Jesus is Lord."

This initiative of our heavenly Father requires a response from us. It is the Father's will and plan that all of us surrender to the Lordship of his Son. The invitation Jesus issued to those to whom he preached—*"Come; follow me."*—he meant for us all. He challenged them and he challenges us to become his disciples.

As we make our decision to claim him as Lord and to follow him, we are actually doing no more than saying "yes" to what was prayed for us when we were baptized. The present rite begins with the priest or deacon, the parents and the sponsors all tracing the sign of the Cross on the forehead of the one to be baptized, setting him/her aside for Jesus.

To follow Jesus as my Lord means placing everything at his disposal: my life, my position, my possessions, my plans, my decisions—everything. He will be the one that I will now submit to in all things. Just as he himself said—*"My food is to do the will of the one who sent me"* (John 4:34)—likewise will my number-one priority become to accomplish his purposes.

I am able to relate to him as a living person because he is risen from the dead, gloriously reigning now at the Father's right hand (Eph 1:20-21) and brought alive for me by the action of the Holy Spirit. I can truly now 'know' him and not just know about him. He is my all.

2. The Blessed Eucharist
Celebrating the Passover meal with his chosen 12 on the eve

of his death on the Cross, Jesus instituted the Eucharist. The Catholic Church has maintained from the beginning its faith in the real presence of Jesus in the Eucharistic elements.

Jesus is present to us as we surrender to him and as the Holy Spirit witnesses within us (John 15:26) to Jesus as risen Saviour. The Master's presence with us in the Eucharist is but another example of the incredible largesse of the Father who, as it were, finds a way to give something to those who already have everything.

Early in its pilgrimage, the Church began reserving one of the consecrated elements, Jesus under the appearance of bread, this Bread of Life (John 6:35), and offering due homage to the Lord present therein in a peculiar way.

The Companions of the Cross believe we are to promote devotion to Jesus in the Blessed Sacrament in every way, including the establishment of perpetual exposition and adoration wherever this may become possible.

3. The Gifts of the Holy Spirit

Jesus, in fulfilling the Father's plan, established the Church (Matt 16:18) to carry on the work of the salvation of mankind after his return to the Father. He did not, however, leave us to do this on our own. He and the Father sent the Holy Spirit (John 14:26) to teach us, to show us the way, and to empower us for the very sizable task commissioned to us. In obedience to the Father, like Jesus, the Holy Spirit came (Acts 2) and remains with us yet.

The Holy Spirit helps us in many ways. St. Paul lists some of these in 1 Corinthians 12. He enumerates nine peculiar charisms: faith, wisdom, knowledge, prophecy, healing, miracles, tongues, discernment of spirits, and interpretation of tongues. These are by no means all the gifts of the Holy Spirit, but they most certainly are among them. He explains these nine, however, as meant specifically for ministry, gifts to be used to further the Lord's work through the Church. These charisms have had an interesting history. Not always very common at every moment of the Church's experience, they have, nonetheless, undergone revival many times, and have been at least minimally present in every age. We are today seeing a renewal in their use as the Lord releases them in greater measure.

The Second Vatican Council re-affirmed their usefulness (*Lumen Gentium* 12) for the present-day ministry of the Church. Pope John Paul II has underscored this several times, most notably in his 1988 apostolic exhortation *Christifideles Laici* (section 20).

The Companions of the Cross enthusiastically endorse the use of the peculiar charisms of the Spirit and will actively seek them, not for their own sake, but for the sake of serving God's people. Though the gifts we speak of may not be in universal use in the Church today, we believe they should be, and we believe the day approaches when they will be. Our conviction is that we, the Church, need all the help we can get.

4. Consecration through the Blessed Mother

We are quite convinced that Jesus' mother, Mary, is presented to us as the best possible, purely human, model of response to the Lord. By her own confession, she was lowly (Luke 1:48), and her degree of emptiness allowed God to do *"great things"* (Luke 1:49) in her.

When we are consecrated to Jesus through her, we are not only asking her to pray for us, we are telling the Lord that we, like her, recognize our own powerlessness to accomplish anything for the kingdom of God—Jesus himself said: *"Without me, you can do nothing"* (John 15:5)—and we are willing, again like the Blessed Virgin, to allow him to do with us whatever he might wish. We say with Mary: *"Let it be done unto me according as you say"* (Luke 1:38).

5. *The Magisterium*

The Magisterium is the name used to identify the official

teaching authority that Jesus has left to the Church. We believe that this office was confided to Peter and the apostles. Jesus, the Good Shepherd, before he ascended to the Father's right hand, appointed Peter as shepherd in his place. Three times, in response to the apostle's confession of love and loyalty to him, Jesus bade him tend the flock (John 21:15-17).

We believe the Pope and the bishops of the Church to be the historical and lawful successors of Peter and the apostles, and to them we pledge our obedience. We recognize the promise of the Lord to provide authentic teaching for his people and to do it through the structures that Jesus himself has initiated.

This submission to lawful authority within the Church will be lived out in our lives as we willingly come under the jurisdiction of our own bishop. We are eager to support him and to take our directions from him.

6. Simplicity

Our sense is that the Lord wants us to move gradually into a much simpler standard of living than is common in North American society today. We are not entirely sure what all the ramifications of this are to be, but we are open to being led by the Lord to receive his ongoing word in this regard and to embrace the program of life he has in mind for us.

We do not think that God is calling us to a radical poverty, but that our style of life is to rely less and less on the material goods that are presented to us in our world today as desirable and even necessary.

7. Ministry

Ours is to be an active community. The Lord has work for us to do. We feel directed by him to minister principally in the inner core areas of our cities and to have a particular care for the 'poor'. The little people of the Gospel story, the *anawim*, to use the Hebrew word, seemed to catch the attention of Jesus much more often than the rich and the famous. He confirmed that one of his principal priorities in ministry was to the marginalized of society when he applied to himself the words of the prophet Isaiah that he had come to *"preach good news to the poor"* (Luke 4:18).

It will be for us a continuing task to discern just what the Lord is directing us to, what segments of 'the poor' we are to be making priority. We will be mindful of the hungry and the homeless, the unemployed, the unwanted, the lonely and unvisited, those in prison, the sick, the elderly, the street people, those in bondage to one addiction or another, the emotionally and mentally disadvantaged, the dying. But we will not want to forget the most needful of all—those who simply do not know the Lord and his good news of life and love. We will make constant efforts to assist people to break the sinful patterns in their lives, those things that separate them from God. In all of our work, we will keep clearly in mind that, no matter how evident people's material and emotional needs may be, the greatest, deepest need every single human being has is for God himself. This is why our underlying thrust in all ministry will be evangelistic, the call to surrender to God and to Jesus, the one he has sent.

There are many kinds of poverty, many divisions of 'the poor'. The Lord wants us to serve them all.

Spirituality

Every community of people called together by the Lord will find that he has fairly specific instructions as to how he wants the members to respond to him. This will comprise and define their **spirituality.**

The Companions of the Cross believe the Lord gave us his basic directions in this regard as we persevered in meeting together in our early days. Though our spirituality is continuing to evolve, we feel the principal elements are already in place.

As we were faithful to the weekly gatherings, as we prayed and listened to the Lord, and as we responded to what we thought he might be saying to us by making commitments to him and to one another, we believe he gently revealed to us the kind of body we were to be. In the light of how God has thus dealt with us, we consider it of vital importance to continue to pray, listen, and respond, and to do it together. We want to be fully available to the Lord for whatever his purposes may be.

It is our deep conviction that God continually looks for individuals and groups of people who are willing to put themselves entirely at his disposal. A Scripture verse that speaks very powerfully to us is 2 Chronicles 16:9. The sacred writer says: *"The eyes of the Lord range constantly across the entire breadth of the earth to search out those who are wholehearted for him so that he might encourage them."*

It is evident, then, that our spirituality is based upon a firm belief that God wishes to be active in the lives of his people, that he is eager to be a participant as his people pilgrim forward, that he languishes unwillingly in the spectator's role to which he is so commonly relegated.

Our spirituality will manifest itself in three principal ways: how we pray, how we live together, and how we attempt to do the Lord's work.

How we pray
Our commitment is to pray both in private and together. Privately, we will, each of us, spend an extended time every day alone with the Lord. We will not be satisfied with our response to God until we have come to the point of giving him a minimum of one hour daily. As well, we will come together each day, in our particular houses, for a time of praise and listening to the Lord. We will proceed on the assumption that God has particular directions for us that he is more than willing to convey. Our common prayer time will include both spontaneous prayer and parts of the Liturgy of the Hours. We will be continually open to all the gifts of the Holy Spirit.

We will also, on a regular basis, pray for needs, both those of others and our own. We will address these directly as they become evident. We will lay hands on those in need if they are present. In any case, we will pray with expectancy and not be surprised if the Lord provides very direct answers to our requests.

How we live together

Our spirituality necessarily includes a shared life. We are to make ourselves available, not only to God, but to one another. Our community living situations will be the main forum in which the Lord will deal with us. While we are to be an active community, not contemplative, we will place great emphasis on how we live together. While we will be a ministry-oriented body, our prior focus will be on our shared life. We strongly believe that, before we can do anything worthwhile for God, we first have to be something together. The Lord will bless our desire to share our lives with one another, but he wants us to know that we will have to work at it.

We will share time together. We will share our goods with one another. We will share our struggles and our joys. This will mean, for each of us, allowing all the others to be who they are. While we will strive to be of one mind and heart around the community's vision, we will recognize that we are all unique, all different in many ways. We will respect each brother's need for personal space and yet, at the same time, be willing to give up our own privacy for the sake of those with whom we share our lives.

We will be committed to working out our differences in open and honest dialogue and learn how to ask for and grant forgiveness.

We believe the Companions of the Cross are to be principally defined by the quality of our life together.

How we work

We will be a community totally committed to the active ministry of the Church. Our call will be principally to our cities, especially to their inner cores. We will undertake the works assigned to us by the bishops of the dioceses to which we are invited. We are to have a special care for the poor, the Lord's little ones, his anawim. We see ourselves pastoring parishes to revival and discipling people to the Lord, to his Church, and to its ministry, and sending them out to bear witness to the Gospel in the marketplace. We will support the Church's commitment to the social gospel and search out the marginalized that we might serve them, meet them at their points of need, whether these be food, shelter, employment, healing, or self-respect. But, we will keep foremost in mind the deepest need that all human beings have: their need for God.

Our principal and over-riding emphasis in ministry, therefore, will be evangelization. We will not, however, stop there. Evangelization, we recognize, is not enough. But we will see it as the first of the Church's tasks, the one without which none of the other ministries will work very well, will not have the effect the Lord wishes them to have.

We will have a special place in our hearts, as well, for alienated Catholics and for youth. But we will be open to taking on any responsibility that the Lord might indicate to us through the bishops of the Church.

We believe the Lord has given us our name, Companions of the Cross, for a reason. The words of Jesus to his disciples strike a responsive chord in our hearts. He said: *"Anyone who does not take up his cross and follow me, cannot be my disciple"* (Luke 14:27). We will not have to search out the Cross. It will find us. And, we believe, we are not to fight it, but to embrace it. It is to be through our embracing of the daily cross that the Lord will best be able to accomplish through us the purposes he has in mind.

There are many authentic spiritualities within the Church. Its history and experience are rich and varied. There are monastic, contemplative, ministry-oriented spiritualities of all kinds. Our particular way of life fits somewhere in the broad spectrum of Church life. We continue to consult the Lord, recognizing that, although he has already set us upon the path he has chosen for us, he undoubtedly has much more to say.

Life Together

Putting lives together is as old as the Church itself. It is deep within the consciousness of the Catholic Church, tracing itself all the way back to the apostolic age. *"Those who believed shared everything in common"* (Acts 2:44). The history of the Church is, in some ways, a history of communities.

The Companions of the Cross feel that they are but a very small link in a long and large chain.

Although we are to be a body committed to the active ministry of the Church, we believe that we will be defined, not so much by the ministry we undertake, but rather by the quality of the life that we will live together. Before we will be able to do anything worthwhile for the Lord together, we will have to be something good together.

We believe the Lord is calling us to become, when it is possible, a society of apostolic life as provided for by the revised Code of Canon Law (canons 731-746). Our present status as a public association of clerics (canons 312-320) does not allow us to structure all of our living situations in the way we would like or as quickly as we would like. Nonetheless, the understanding leadership of Archbishop Plourde is already making it possible for us to conduct some experiments. We hope to be sensitive to the promptings of the Holy Spirit as we search out the structures of shared life the Lord may want us to embrace. We will begin with something like the following:

- morning prayer fairly early, around 7am ... a time comprised of three basic components—spontaneous praise and song, silence, morning prayer from the Liturgy
of the Hours ... open at any time to the use of spiritual gifts
... 30–40 minutes;

- evening meal preceded by a shorter period of common prayer, possibly the Church's official evening prayer ... 10–5 minutes;

- one Saturday evening a month an extended time together, a 'house' night which would include the evening meal and further activities, perhaps based on something like the Lord's Day celebration employed by some of the covenant communities;

- the other Saturday evenings—an openness to spending the time together, always allowing for a brother's possible ministry involvement or need for quiet time ... remembering one of the earliest words received at the brothers' meetings—'be creative in finding ways to spend time together.'

- a common day off, probably Monday, which would make it possible for the brothers, on occasion, to spend time together in recreation and relaxation.

The above household routine would, of course, be supplemented by spiritual direction, weekly share group, and weekly community meeting. It is important that we find the balance that can give us the support we need while allowing us sufficient time and freedom both for the ministry we undertake and the time we need to ourselves.

We would hope to get used to being accountable to one another for our participation in the life of the community. We would make commitments to one another to be present at all exercises and make our regrets to the house superior for any time we might have to miss. As we become used to the structure of our life together, we will get to experience the support simply of being together, present both to the Lord and to one another. Any time a brother has to be missing, we will 'feel' his absence and look forward to the time when he can be with us again.

St. Paul seems to be writing a useful blueprint for us. *"Because you are God's chosen ones, holy and beloved, clothe*

yourselves with heartfelt mercy, with kindness, humility, meekness, and patience. Bear with one another; forgive whatever grievances you have against one another. Forgive as the Lord has forgiven you. Over all these virtues, put on the love which binds the rest together and makes them perfect. Christ's peace must reign in your hearts, since, as members of the one body, you have been called to that peace. Dedicate yourselves to thankfulness. Let the word of Christ, in all its richness, dwell within you. In wisdom made perfect, instruct and admonish one another. Sing gratefully to God from your hearts psalms, hymns, and inspired songs. Whatever you do, whether in word or in action, do it in the name of the Lord Jesus. Give thanks to God the Father through him"
(Col 3:12-17).

And St. Peter has a word to add. *"Above all, let your love for one another be constant, for love covers a multitude of sins. Be mutually hospitable without complaining. As generous distributors of God's manifold grace, put your gifts at the service of one another each in the measure he has received"* (1 Pet 4:8-10).

We believe very firmly that what we are doing has been initiated by the Lord himself. We pray that we don't take it off the track he has set it on. We are convinced, in addition, that this little enterprise is the same kind of thing God wants to establish in every place, that it is very much at the heart of what he wants to do in the renewal of the diocesan priesthood.

There is no real reason, we believe, that every diocese couldn't function as a community. Why could the presbyterium not meet regularly with the bishop for teaching and becoming of one mind with regard to pastoral priorities? Why could priests not live together in households of four or five and work in different places? It might be difficult for priests and people to get used to, but it's possible. And the benefits would be tremendous. To priests and people alike.

Living together in supportive relationships can serve as the protection we need against the many hazards of ministry we experience. It's time to end the isolation priests have been living in for too long.

Putting our lives together may not always be easy. It can be fairly threatening to become as vulnerable as community will demand of us. But it is worth doing. It is one of God's basic works.

The unity of our life together will authenticate the Gospel we proclaim and give it power.

Positional Statement

[With the approval of the Apostolic See the Companions of the Cross were erected as a Society of Apostolic Life by Archbishop Marcel Gervais on May 3, 2003. This Positional Statement was the earliest form of what is now the Constitutions and Rules of the Companions of the Cross.]

We, the Companions of the Cross, are a public association of clerics as allowed in the revised Code of Canon Law, canons 312 and following. Our status became official by decree of the Most Reverend Joseph-Aurele Plourde, Archbishop of Ottawa, effective February 11, 1988, feast of Our Lady of Lourdes. We are now, therefore, a body of priests, candidates for the priesthood, and men committed to living single for the Lord in a brotherhood.

The vision we believe the Lord has given us rests upon two major components: God's wisdom and God's power. In order to be in touch with his wisdom and to allow his power to be ministered through us, we sense we have to be fully abandoned to him and fully available to him as well. This will involve, we believe, embracing the Cross. Just as Jesus was obedient to the Father's will right to the end, so must we.

We are committed to seeking the Lord's wisdom, his directive 'now' word, in all things, and to making no important moves without it. This will often involve us, therefore, in an extensive waiting upon the Lord. In addition, we are in very good touch with our own inability to do the Lord's work without his immediate participation. We feel we have a good understanding of Jesus' words: *"Without me, you can do noth-*

ing" (John 15:5). Without God's power, our efforts will be in vain. But with it, all things will be possible (Luke 1:37).

While recognizing the reality that we can get it wrong, we believe we have the 'wisdom' of God directing us to embrace a number of clear priorities.

1. Each of us is to declare himself personally under the Lordship of Jesus Christ and to live this commitment out daily in conscious submission to him as Saviour and King.

2. We believe the Lord wants us to promote in a very positive way an understanding and appreciation of the Holy Eucharist, a great reverence for Jesus, reserved in the Blessed Sacrament, and even to establish, wherever possible, perpetual adoration.

3. We are to anticipate in our lives the operation of all the ministry gifts of the Holy Spirit, including the charisms listed by St. Paul in 1 Corinthians 12.

4. We believe the Lord is directing us to place high priority on the ministry of evangelization as outlined by Pope Paul VI in his encyclical, *Evangelii Nuntiandi*, an evangelization based upon the dynamic in which, when the Lord's call is proclaimed and a person responds by saying an effective 'yes', God himself touches the person and begins a transformation that can see him/her come alive in faith in a whole new way and be set on fire for the Lord.

5. We are to recognize the powerful, prophetic ministry the Father has given to the Church in these times, of Mary, mother of Jesus and mother of the Church, Queen of Peace, as well as her apparent special assignment from God to give leadership to the renewal of the priesthood; and, in consequence of these, to be consecrated to her Immaculate Heart, standing as she does before Jesus— totally empty, fully available to him, willing to be led by the Holy Spirit in all things.

6. We are to have a particular loyalty to the Holy Father and the Magisterium of the Church, a loyalty that will be lived out in loyal obedience to our local bishop, while we continue to believe that Pope John Paul II is especially chosen by God to shepherd his people in this critical age.

7. We are to embrace a certain simplicity of lifestyle, not only because we believe this to be integral to the Gospel, but also because we are convinced the Church must take a radical, prophetic stand in the midst of a society almost totally secular in its goals, a world so unhappily divided between rich and poor nations.

8. We are to live a common life, one in which we can, in the Lord, affirm, support, and challenge one another, submitting to the community for discernment and counsel all major decisions in our individual lives. This agenda will entail investing a lot of ourselves and our time in developing our life together.

9. We are to undertake as our principal works, ministries to youth, to alienated Catholics, and to the poor (the desperate, those in bondage, the addicted, the abused, the hungry, the sick, the homeless, the lonely, the isolated, those in prison, the abandoned, the jobless, the runaways, the street people, and those who are the poorest of the poor: those who do not know Jesus and his love).

10. We are to be a community whose active ministry is to be balanced by a strong commitment, on a daily basis, to regular times of prayer, both in common and in private.

11. We are to be open to taking on responsibility fo downtown parishes, attempting to pastor them to a significant degree of renewal, calling parishioners forth in this exciting day of the development of lay ministry and preparing them to work at our sides in our assigned tasks.

12. We are to expect a day to come, in the not-too-distant future, when, the Lord having added to our number, we will be able to accept calls to minister in places other than Ottawa, our home base.

13. We are to make ourselves available to priests and seminarians in any way we can, providing whatever ministries of hospitality and healing seem indicated and possible.

14. We are to anticipate the gathering of a group of women around this same vision in an autonomous sisterhood which will share our ministry, and also a group of lay people who, while developing and maintaining their own independence, will associate themselves with us in some way for the building up of the Lord's kingdom on earth.

It is our feeling that the type of community into which we believe the Lord is drawing us is part of his plan for the renewal of the diocesan priesthood and intended by him to develop in all population centres. We believe people in many different places have already heard the same call and that we are to be in relationship with them as the Lord sets up a network to promote his plan. On our part, we believe we are to bring the vision to other places when he gives us the word, but that our present task is to start it now here in Ottawa.

The Lay Associates
[What follows is the first vision statement for the Lay Associates. Since that time it has been revised and modified to further accommodate the lay faithful. The most recent version may be found at www.companionscross.org]

Almost from the very beginning, that point at which we felt certain the Lord was calling for a new community of priests, we had the clear sense that he would call together, as well, a body of lay people to "associate themselves with us in some way", as our positional statement puts it.

Accordingly, in September of 1986, we opened up the regular Friday night meeting of the brothers to all those interested in some kind of association with us. Within a year, over one hundred people were joining us as we praised God and sought his word. While this has been a wonderful source of support and encouragement to us, we have had a persistent notion that the vision for the lay association remained incomplete. It was not until the spring of 1989 that we were relatively certain that the full description (which follows) of the role of our lay associates was substantially in place.

We believe the lay group is to be based on the vision of the Companions of the Cross, combining this with a sound spirituality for the lay person, for men and women who are eager to be disciples of Jesus Christ in the fullest sense of the word. The living out of this spirituality would lead to involvement of some kind in the ministry of the community. It would thus bring together people, married and single, young (minimum age—16) and old, discerning and settled.

The associates would embrace the underlying concepts of the wisdom and the power of God upon which the vision of the Companions of the Cross rests. They would be open to being called to assist in the community's prior ministries —to evangelize and to serve the poor, alienated Catholics, and youth—and would identify with the community's:

1. Surrender to the Lordship of Jesus,
2. furthering of devotion to the Eucharist,
3. use of all the ministry gifts of the Holy Spirit,
4. consecration to Jesus through the Immaculate Heart of Mary,
5. loyalty to the Magisterium of the Church, and
6. simplicity of lifestyle.

This spirituality will be lived out in a series of very practical ways. The lay associate will:

1. Spend an extended time each day in personal prayer;
2. read Scripture daily;
3. participate in the Mass and the Sacraments frequently;
4. be consecrated to Jesus through Mary;
5. in discernment with the community, undertake some kind of ministry;
6. keep a spiritual journal;
7. tithe;
8. be a member of a share group that meets at least every two weeks;
9. make daily intercession for the intentions of the community;
10. attend the annual retreat;
11. fast weekly;
12. take part in the periodic celebrations of the association.

We expect that our lay associates will make annual commitments to live out the spirituality. Before undertaking to do it for the first time, however, some kind of preparation will be in order. A series of teachings will periodically, therefore, be made available.

We feel we need to be open to further developments which, at this time, remain unforeseen. We must always allow the Lord to move ahead with his plans and not assume that we already have the finished product. We would want, for one thing, to encourage household living situations and be ready to see the possibility that some people might sense a call to enter with one another more extensive, covenanted relationships.

The lay associates will be served by a board of co-ordinators which will include at least a chairperson and directors of ministries, share groups, and teachings.

The lay associates will be further served by the Companions of the Cross newsletter which, while being sent to all interested people, will be directed principally to communicating with them and dealing with their needs.

With the addition of lay associates from various walks of life, we can see the Companions of the Cross developing as a real spiritual family with workable support structures for all those taking part.

Living out the Commitment

Following are the components of the spirituality that we feel the Lord would want associates of the community to embrace.

1. Personal prayer

The highest possible priority must be placed upon the individual's daily quiet time with the Lord. It is here that the Lord is enabled to deal most effectively with his adopted son/daughter.

We consider an hour a day to be essential, the minimum required for a person to grow in an intimate relationship with God. However, we concede that someone who is just beginning to pray seriously may have difficulty in finding and spending an hour in prayer on a regular basis. We encourage those who are starting to set a realistic goal and to strive to be faithful to that while gradually adding to the time as it becomes possible.

We want to make a distinction between prayer and 'prayers'. The latter would be those composed by others and recited by us. The Rosary would be an example of this. Many find it an invaluable assistance in their relationship with the Lord. It can have a very gentle, calming effect upon the human spirit, disposing us more effectively to hear the Lord.

We recommend it. But what we have in mind for our personal time with the Lord is spontaneous prayer, speaking to the Lord in our own words. And, since prayer is meant to be communication between God and me, I have to give him a chance to speak, too. This will mean that part of my prayer time will be spent simply trying to listen to the Lord. We will say with Samuel: *"Speak, Lord. Your servant is listening"* (1 Sam 3:10). As we persevere daily with a time of silence, we will probably begin to get a gradually clearer idea of how the Lord wants to communicate with us.

2. Sacred Scripture

The Bible is the written word of God, and *"all Scripture is inspired by God and is useful for teaching, for reproof, correction, and training in holiness"* (2 Tim 3:16). A quiet reading of the inspired word can be made a most useful part of personal prayer time.

In any case, we strongly encourage a systematic reading of Scripture every day. For one who is just beginning to open up to the treasures of the written word, we suggest a programmed approach. Consultation could be had with one or more of the many good Bible study guides. Attendance at a solid Scripture teaching series can also go a long way to getting us well started.

The Scriptures are an irreplaceable compendium of God's word to us. He can speak to us through them. One of the most consistent testimonies coming from people who have just surrendered their lives to the Lord for the first time in any serious way is the manner in which the Bible seems simply to jump alive for them. A previously unexperienced hunger for God's word begins to motivate them to get into the Scriptures and learn the ways of God. Part of our quiet time with the Lord should include some prayerful reading of the Bible.

3. Mass and Sacraments

Jesus commanded the Church to make present again and again his saving sacrifice upon the Cross. He gave us the Eucharist. The Church has responded faithfully and has developed the practice of celebrating the mysteries of the Lord every day. We urge all associates to take advantage of every opportunity to offer Mass and receive Holy Communion, the very body and blood of the Lord (1 Cor 11:27).

As well, we recommend a regular celebration of the Lord's forgiveness in the Sacrament of Reconciliation. Every month or two would seem to be a desirable goal.

The Eucharist and the Sacraments can be powerfully anointed moments in our lives as we soldier on with the Lord to our eternal goal.

We want to pray, it is obvious, with the Church. We will celebrate the sacred mysteries together as the Lord leads us and will include the Liturgy of the Hours, even done in a communal setting as this becomes possible for us.

4. Journaling

A spiritual journal is not a diary. It is the place where I record my questions to the Lord, my hopes, my fears, my apologies, my frustrations. It is likewise the place where I jot down what I think he may be saying to me.

Many people are reluctant to keep a journal because they fear the time required will be too demanding. It doesn't have to be. Some days, a line or two will suffice. Some days perhaps nothing at all. Other times, as inspiration seems to take over, longer entries will be appropriate.

The journal is a valuable record for me as to how the Lord is directing my life. Reviewing it from time to time can help to keep me on track. Looking backwards is very often the reminder I need about God's now word for me. Without a journal, that can be very difficult, next to impossible.

5. Ministry

We expect that all of our associates will undertake some form of ministry. What the Lord has given us is to be shared, not hoarded.

However, in order to keep things in balance, each one's ministry is to be discerned with the community. There is an ever-present temptation for those who are on fire for the Lord to undertake too much. Over-extension can lead to frustration and burn-out, things the Lord wants us to avoid.

In the case of parents with young children, it is likely that most of their ministry, perhaps all of it, will be at home.

6. Tithing

God's Old Testament people had a clear word from him on what he wanted them to give to his work. It was 10% off the top of everything. Jesus didn't change the teaching. In fact, he encouraged an even more generous response.

We urge our associates to enter into the fascinating world of the tithe. For those for whom it is new, we suggest setting at first a more modest goal and moving gradually toward the Lord's 10%. But, it is imperative to set it at a definite percentage. And the percentage we set is in relationship, not to our net earnings, but related to our gross intake.

As to the direction of the tithe, we think it should be worked out in consultation with the Lord. (For a fuller explanation, see the chapter on "Tithing".)

7. Share Groups

It is important for each associate to be a member of a small group, a half dozen people or so, with whom he/she can share the struggles of life and give and receive ministry for personal needs.

The group meeting, taking place at least every two weeks, will ordinarily last about an hour and a half.

8. Intercession

Part of our personal quiet time with the Lord, will be spent bringing before him the needs of the community. The ordained and professed brothers are on the firing line full-time every day and can expect the regular attacks that all those in the midst of spiritual battle will undergo. What a blessing for them to know that they are held before the Lord daily by a large group of lay associates.

As some of the associates themselves are called into more and more ministry time, they, too, will need much prayer support. And all, members of the community and the association alike, are urged to pray daily for one another's needs.

9. Retreat

Once a year, the associates will gather for a Friday to Sunday retreat. This will be a time to worship and seek the Lord together, more fully develop the relationships among members, and to receive good teaching.

10. Fasting

The fast is a long-neglected area of response to God's call upon the Church. We would like to help resurrect it. It is a powerful intercessory tool before the Lord, particularly when done in corporate fashion.

Our recommendation is that we undertake a fast on Friday, the day when Jesus achieved his (and our) victory over sin and death.

There are many ways to fast. Not all can manage 24 hours on bread and water, or on water alone. But different modifications are possible: skipping a meal or two; no food between sunrise and sunset; cutting down on portions or on favoured items. For those whose medical situations do not allow them to tamper with their food programs, other forms of fasting are possible in the areas of television, radio, or newspapers.

Coming voluntarily away from some of the things we normally depend on makes it possible for us to come into more dependence on God.

11. Communal celebrations

We plan to have, annually, four or five official gatherings of the association, possibly in conjunction with some of the First Fridays. These will normally include the celebration of the Eucharist and some time of fellowship.

As the Lord's people pray and play together, he is better able to mould them into the cohesive bodies he wants to call together in our day.

CHAPTER SIX

Mary, the First Companion of the Cross

The following piece was written originally as an apologetic for the role of our Blessed Mother. It finds its base completely in Scriptural references and implications because it was aimed at those who deny to her a present function in the Church and the world precisely because they fail to find justification for such a thing in the Bible.

But we offer this revision of the original here because we believe the Lord wants us to accord her a very special place in the community. After all, she stood at the foot of Jesus' Cross, faithful to the last. She was a Companion of the Cross long before any of us.

That all may be one

The saddest fact about Christianity is that it is divided. This has never been God's idea. We have taken our divisions too long for granted.

Surely, Jesus' most fervent plea to the Father is his prayer for us to be one. *"I do not pray for them alone. I pray also for those who will believe in me through their word, so that all may be one as you, Father, are in me, and I in you. I pray that they may be one in us so that the world may believe that you have sent me"* (John 17:20-22). This is a cry from the heart, obviously.

The prayer is fervent, to be certain. But the implication is, to say the least, unsettling. It would seem that the principal authenticating feature of our testimony to the Gospel is to be our unity, our oneness with one another. If we are one, then, we can expect the Lord to invest our witness with power, the power it will take to produce conversion to Jesus in those who hear. We do not possess such power ourselves. It comes only from God. Only he can touch and capture a human heart.

But, if we are not one? What about that? The distressing conclusion has to be that our proclamation of the Good News will lack the power God wants it to have.

The Church has done great work over the centuries. But we haven't even come close to taking the world for the kingdom of God. Why not? We are divided. That's why. To the degree that the Church is fragmented, to that degree is our work compromised. To the degree that we are one, to that degree our work is effective.

The unity of the Body of Christ is crucial. It is not an option or a nice idea.

God's work is unity. The Father, the Son, and the Holy Spirit are perfectly one. The Father calls all of us into perfect unity, too, so that we may share his life. His work is unity. Division is the work of someone else, Satan, our enemy from the start. And he's been at the task of dividing Christians right from the foundation of the Church. We have only to read St. Paul's letters to the Corinthians and the Galatians to know the truth of that.

Satan's work is division. He's very good at it. And he has been very successful. The Church, founded at such cost, is badly divided.

There are many things that divide us. Cardinal Suenens

said some years ago, and with considerable insight, that two of the greatest barriers to Christian unity are Peter and Mary.

The Pope, the successor to Peter, the head of the apostolic band, is meant to be a visible sign of the unity of God's people. He is not seen as such.

Mary, Jesus' own mother, is intended by God to be a factor of unity within the Church. Like any mother, one of the best things she can do is hold the family together. But, like Peter, her role is not well understood.

What is the solution to be? Is there a solution at all? Are we, as Catholics, expected to set aside the roles of Mary and Peter in the interests of a wider unity? Are non-Catholics expected simply to accept the teachings of the Catholic Church? Neither of these seems likely to happen in a hurry. Setting aside the role of Peter for the purposes of this study, let us pursue the role of Mary.

What is the best route to take? When I undertook preparation of the original talk, my sense was that the Lord was pointing to the Scriptures. I think he still is. While Christians may disagree on any number of things, there is a firm, unwavering agreement on the part of all believers in the authority of the inspired, written word of God.

If we go there together, if we go prayerfully in reverence for the Lord's word and with respect for one another, will he not teach us how to become one?

Model

We all need examples to emulate. St. Paul said as much. *"You know,"* he said to the Thessalonians, *"how you are supposed to imitate us"* (2 Thess 3:7). And to the Corinthians he said: *"Be imitators of me as I am of Christ"* (1 Cor 11:1).

It would be difficult to find a better example to follow than Mary, the mother of the Redeemer.

She freely submitted to the plan of the Father and held nothing back. *"Let it be done unto me,"* she replied to the angel Gabriel, *"according to your word"* (Luke 1:37). She could hardly have foreseen all that this would lead her to, but she offered herself nonetheless.

She deflected all praise away from herself, giving the glory only to God. *"He has looked upon the lowliness of his servant. The Lord, who is mighty, has done great things for me. Holy is his name"* (Luke 1:48-49).

She was a woman of willing and humble service. Upon learning about the unexpected pregnancy of her cousin, Elizabeth, she set out at once on a mission of mercy. She stayed with the older woman and helped her through the delivery of her child (Luke 1:39).

She was sensitive and compassionate. When the wine ran out at the wedding in Cana (John 2), she sought to save the host a major embarrassment by enlisting the aid of her son.

She was prayerful, contemplative even. She *"treasured all these things and reflected upon them in her heart"* (Luke 2:19).

She was, perhaps above all, loyal and faithful. Just as Jesus followed obediently his Father's will, even to the Cross, Mary followed her son and stood by him there, close to him in his terrible hour, right to the end. While most of his disciples fled, she remained. "Near the Cross of Jesus, there stood his mother" (John 19:25).

She was one of the body of believers, a member of the Church, and persevered with the others in prayer as they waited for the fulfillment of the Father's promise, the coming of the Holy Spirit (Acts 1:14).

Mary, through the power of the Holy Spirit, brought Jesus forth into the world. Surely, a better description of the mission

of each Christian could not be found. We, each of us, are to cooperate with the Holy Spirit and bring Jesus to others.

She gave up her autonomy, her independence, to become total dependence. She became completely empty so that God could fill her and do great things in her (Luke 1:47).

As a model of response to the Gospel, Mary's equal is hard to find.

Highly favoured daughter

"Rejoice, O highly favoured daughter. The Lord is with you. Blessed are you among women" (Luke 1:28). These are the words with which the angel Gabriel greeted Mary as he came to announce to her that she was called to be the mother of the long-awaited Saviour.

Favoured indeed! When Mary said 'yes' to the plan of God, while already daughter of the Father, she became, as well, mother of the Son, and spouse of the Holy Spirit. She entered into, at his invitation, a uniquely intimate relationship with God. We are called to intimacy with God, but none of us has the same relationship with him as she. She is highly favoured and blessed above us all.

Elizabeth seemed to take up where Gabriel left off. She, too, greeted Mary with words of high compliment. *"Blessed are you among women,"* she said, repeating the words of the angel, *"and blessed is the fruit of your womb. But who am I that the mother of my Lord should come to me?"* (Luke 1:42-43). Elizabeth, speaking obviously at the inspiration of the Holy Spirit, was simply recognizing what should be evident to us all. Mary stands out among all women, among all humankind for that matter, as the one favoured in a way that none of the rest of us can ever be.

Minister

Mary's principal role in life was to give birth to Jesus, to be his mother. This she did. But this is not all she did. She was busy doing other things, too. She did things for other people. She engaged herself, at God's behest no doubt, in ministry.

Right after her encounter with Gabriel, the messenger of the Lord, *"she went with haste into the hill country, to a town of Judah"* (Luke 1:39). She undertook an errand of mercy. She made herself available to Elizabeth, her cousin, who, at the promise of God, had herself conceived a son. Elizabeth was *"advanced in years"* (Luke 1:7), had come to a time in life when child-bearing would be very difficult. Mary went to help. It was to be a ministry of presence and service.

But God had additional plans. As soon as Mary greeted her cousin, the latter was *"filled with the Holy Spirit,"* and the child, as St. Luke says, *"leaped in her womb"* (Luke 1:41). When she heard Mary's words, Elizabeth responded with a *"loud cry"* (Luke 1:42) and returned a greeting to her. This is ministry of another kind. The Lord used Mary to minister the Holy Spirit to Elizabeth and to her unborn child, John, as well.

At Cana, there is ministry of yet another kind. When the wine reserves ran out, Mary, probably a good friend of the host family, took the matter to her son. When Jesus seemed unimpressed by the situation and disinclined to respond, she persisted and simply advised the servants to *"Do whatever he tells you"* (John 2:5). Jesus, as we know, did take the matter in hand. He, in fact, performed his *"first sign"* (John 2:11).

This is, of course, a ministry of intercession. We are all called to be intercessors, to pray for the world, the Church, and one another, to the Father through Jesus. Mary did that. She knew where the power was.

Presentation

The three ideas we have just examined—Mary as model, Mary as favoured, Mary as minister in her own day—are hardly controversial. There won't be much division around those suggestions.

The differences of opinion will ordinarily begin at the implication that she has a present role in the Church, that she is active now. What can we look to in Scripture to give us a clue about this?

Suppose we start with a look at the presentation of Jesus in the Temple.

Joseph and Mary were faithful members of God's chosen people, Israel. Joseph, described by the evangelist, St. Matthew, as "a just man" (Matt 1:19), was obedient to the Lord as well. On three different occasions, he faithfully followed the directions God was giving him through his dreams (Matt 1:20, 2:13,

2:19). Mary, of course, was *"the highly favoured one"* (Luke 1:28) and *"blessed among women"* (Luke 1:42).

They were zealous for the Law, keen to fulfill all of its prescriptions. They had Jesus circumcised on the eighth day, just as the Law commanded (Luke 1:21). And, after the proper time had elapsed, they took the child to the Temple to present him to the Lord, just as the Law indicated it should be done. *"And when the day came for them to be purified as laid down by the Law of Moses, they took him up to Jerusalem to present him to the Lord, observing what stands written in the Law of the Lord, and also to offer a sacrifice, in accordance with what is said in the Law of the Lord, a pair of turtle doves or two young pigeons"* (Luke 2:22-24).

While they were at the Temple, *"an upright and devout man"* (Luke 2:25) came up to them. This was Simeon, and *"the Holy Spirit rested upon him"* (Luke 2:25). He had been told by the Lord that he would not die until he saw the Messiah, the anointed one who was to come (Luke 2:26). He was led by the Spirit that day to the Temple and, when he saw Jesus, he recognized him at once as the Christ of God. Simeon thereupon praised God for the fulfillment of his promise and prayed a blessing for Joseph and Mary (Luke 2:26-34).

As St. Luke tells it, Simeon then addressed some words to Jesus' mother. *"You see this child? He is destined for the fall and the rising of many in Israel. He shall be a sign of contradiction, a sign rejected—and a sword shall pierce your own soul, too—so that the secret thoughts of many may be laid bare"* (Luke 2:34-35).

He was speaking, of course, about the Cross. Jesus would bring the authentic good news of life and confirm it with signs, works of healing and deliverance. He would do everything that his Father would tell him to do. But, because he would call for repentance, for people to change the sinful patterns of their lives, and because he would not be the temporal deliverer most people were looking for, he would be rejected. Because he would issue a strong call to the religious leaders to change their ways, they would plot to do away with him. And they would succeed. He would go to the Cross. It would become the ultimate sign of contradiction, the stumbling block (1 Cor 1:23) that would bar the way to life for many while it opened life's gates for others. The 'secret thoughts' would be uncovered. People would be cut to the heart. They would respond to the call of the Gospel and be saved.

But what of the words of Simeon that refer particularly to Mary? He said she would suffer, too. She came to know the truth of his prophecy when she stood beneath the Cross. The sword of sorrow was plunged deep. She is well called the Mother of Sorrows.

But there is an implication here that escapes, perhaps, the unpractised eye. Jesus' sufferings would have profound effect, Simeon says. Salvation would become possible for the whole world. But, as he puts it, Mary's sufferings would be joined to his. And for the same purpose. And just as Jesus' passion and death would not be limited to his day, but have effect in every age, so, perhaps, would hers.

Do we have a hint here that there was to be an ongoing ministry for Jesus' mother, that Mary's presence in salvation history would not be limited to her lifetime here on earth? I would suggest that the word of God leans in that direction.

As she ministered, then, the Holy Spirit to Elizabeth and John, would she continue to do so throughout the centuries? As she intervened at Cana, would she do it again and again? Could well be. After all, Simeon did say that she would suffer so that others might benefit.

God's agents

We know that the Lord can and does use his angels, at times, to minister to his people on earth. Scripture is replete with references to this reality. But can he use believers who die to do the same kind of thing?

There are some Christians who claim he does not do this. They say it would contradict his explicit word in Deuteronomy 18, which rules out relating to the dead. It would border on the occult, they say.

I guess we would have to have a look at what happened on the mountain of the transfiguration (Matt 17:1-8). Moses and Elijah appeared to Jesus there. We would not want to call their participation an instance of the occult. Would we not have to say that the Father can use anybody he wants, anybody who's on his side that is, to accomplish his purposes?

Besides, Jesus changed the whole definition of death. When he went to Bethany on the occasion of Lazarus' death (there was an interesting outcome to that one, for sure), he spoke reassuring words to Martha. *"I am the resurrection and the life,"* he said. *"If anyone believe in me, even if he die, he will live. Whoever lives and believes in me will never die at all"* (John 11:25-26). He turned death, which looks for all the world like the end of the line, into a doorway leading to eternal life. Those who die in the Lord cannot correctly be referred to as dead. They live with him.

We are accustomed to calling this the Communion of Saints. The Body of Christ is alive both in this life and beyond. If the Father wants some kind of interaction among us, that is really no problem to him. It shouldn't be a problem for us, either.

Does Mary continue to minister? There doesn't seem to be any good reason why not.

Music and Incense

We know that there are people in heaven now with the Lord. They, with us, await the return of Jesus to earth, the event which will herald the resurrection of the dead and the translation of God's people into glory. We know for sure the repentant thief is there, one of the ones who was crucified with Jesus. *"Jesus,"* he pleaded, *"remember me when you come into your kingdom."* The response he received is one we'd all like to hear. *"I assure you:"* Jesus replied, *"this day you will be with me in paradise"* (Luke 23:42-43).

But, if there are people in heaven now, what are they doing? There is a Scripture verse that seems to speak directly to this question. It is from the book of Revelation. It occurs in chapter five. Jesus is portrayed as the victorious Lamb of God, worthy to receive honour and glory and praise. In the highly symbolic language typical of the apocalyptic genre, the writer, John, continues to describe his vision. *"The Lamb came forward to take the scroll from the right hand of the one sitting on the throne. As he took it, the four animals prostrated themselves before him. So, too, did the twenty-four elders. Each one was holding a harp and had a golden bowl, full of incense, made of the prayers of the saints"* (Rev 5:7-8).

The symbols may need explaining. Jesus, of course, is the Lamb. The scroll is the plan of God, the book wherein the names of the redeemed are recorded. The one on the throne is the Father. The four animals may represent characteristics of God's people when we're at our best. Spoken of elsewhere in Scripture, the animals—the lion, the eagle, the ox, and the one who has the likeness of a man—symbolize strength, swiftness, courage, and intelligence. The 24 elders are all the leadership of the people of God. It is 12 (Old Testament patriarchs) plus 12 (New Testament apostles). The harp, a musical instrument, represents the praise they, the ones in heaven, are rendering to Jesus. We are told specifically what the bowl of incense represents. These are prayers going to the Father through Jesus. Whose prayers? The prayers of the saints. The saints are God's people, the Church, on earth. The New Testament uses the term 'saints' to refer exclusively to those of us on earth.

With all of that having been said, are there a couple of things clear to us? Can we see that there are people in heaven now with the Lord? Is it clear that they are active, involved not only with God, but active on our behalf as well?

Mary is, we would have to believe, one of those with the Lord. Is she acting on our behalf? Seems to be no question about it at all.

Cana

We are all fairly familiar with the story of the wedding at Cana. "Three days later (after the calling of Nathanael), there was a wedding at Cana in Galilee. The mother of Jesus was there. And Jesus himself, along with his disciples, had also been invited" (John 2:1-2).

Cana was a sleepy little town, probably about 20 miles north of Nazareth, a considerable journey in those days, more than a day's travel. It was certainly a long way to go for a wedding. It seems likely, then, that the family in Cana, the family hosting the wedding celebration, were very good friends of Mary, perhaps even relatives.

Mary, having committed herself to being present at the festivities, was probably doing what so many out-of-town invitees would tend to do in such a situation. She was probably busying herself helping out wherever she could. Could we see her poking around in the pantry, seeing to the trays of goodies and so on? The affairs of the kitchen and the service of food and hospitality have long been very much a woman's concern.

Was she, then, in a position to notice the unexpected depletion of the wine? Was she, perhaps, a party to the hurried conferences about what could be done to save the situation? Her sensitivity would, no doubt lead her to feel badly about the host's mortification, the extreme embarrassment he and his family would experience at this failure at hospitality, something on which the Jewish people placed such a high premium.

It was probably in a context like this, therefore, that Mary thought about approaching her son. Would it be appropriate? She knew he could provide a solution. Setting aside her hesitations, she gave it a try. "*They have no wine,*" she said to him (John 2:3).

His response seemed, at first, to indicate that she had misread the situation. He would shortly, of course, solve the problem. But, his words merit a close look. Giving it a literal translation, his reply was as follows: *"Woman, what to you and to me? My hour has not yet come"* (John 2:4).

He addresses his mother as 'woman'. Although this would be unacceptable today in our language, it was an ordinary, polite form of address for the people of Jesus' time and place. Jesus is recorded as using it several times. *"Woman,"* he asked Mary Magdalene, *"why are you weeping?"* (John 20:15). When he spoke to the Canaanite woman, he said: *"Woman, you have great faith. Let your wish be granted"* (Matt 15:28). There was nothing unusual about it.

There is a problem, however. It would be unusual for a son to use the term 'woman' when speaking to his own mother. Why, then, would Jesus call his mother 'woman'?

Does it evoke for us, perhaps, the earliest story in the whole Bible, the story of the fall of mankind? After Adam's fall, the Lord addressed a few well chosen words to the devil. *"I will put enmity,"* he said, *"between you and the* woman, *between your seed and hers. You will lie in wait for his heel, and he will crush your head"* (Gen 3:15). Was the Lord saying that he intended, at some point, to raise up a woman whose offspring would bring final defeat upon Satan's head? The woman's 'seed', would vanquish mankind's enemy once and for all.

The 'seed', the one who would be our champion, defeating our implacable foe, has turned out, obviously, to be Jesus. The woman, his mother, is just as obviously Mary.

Getting back to Jesus' response to his mother's comment about the wine, we have other questions to ask. When he suggests that the problem should be no real concern of his, we can, perhaps, understand and agree. But when he suggests that it should not concern her either, we have a question. If she has been involved behind the scenes, it is natural for her to be concerned. And yet, he almost seems to chide her for wanting to interfere. There must be something more behind his question than, at first glance, appears.

Jesus then says that his hour has not yet come. What hour is he talking about? Is he referring, as we would ordinarily suspect, to his time to begin performing signs? It doesn't seem so. He goes right ahead anyway to work a sign on behalf of the family in Cana. What hour, then?

We have to look at how the evangelist, John, quotes Jesus as using the word 'hour' itself. It has a very specific meaning. There is only one real 'hour' in Jesus' life. John, the beloved disciple, says in another place: *"It was before the festival of the Passover, and Jesus knew that the hour had come for him to pass from this world to the Father"* (John 13:1). That was it, then. The 'hour' Jesus refers to at Cana, is the 'hour' that will come later, that time when he will go to the Cross to fulfill the Father's plan for the redemption of the human race. That will be the time when he will take on the enemy of mankind in mortal combat and defeat him by the Cross. That's what he means by the 'hour'.

Why does he mention it at Cana, though? What does it have to do with this situation of seemingly minor importance? Why else, except to say something very specific to his mother? She, the 'woman', will be present at his 'hour'. She will be involved in it, as Simeon has prophesied. In fact, at the Cross, he will call her 'woman' again, the only other recorded time that he will do this.

Can we put some meaning to it? Is Jesus saying at Cana that Mary's ministry of intercession on behalf of God's people is not really supposed to begin until the battle of Calvary has been won? Is he saying that this actually should wait until he has given her, finally, to the Church? Is he indicating that she is to receive an added role in the plan of salvation, a special role of co-operation in his mission. Simeon has seemed to suggest just that.

If this is so, it would not be the last time that the Lord would choose one of *"the weak things of this world in order to confound the strong"* (1 Cor 1:27).

The Hour Arrives

Jesus said: *"A man can have no greater love than to lay*

down his life for his friends" (John 15:13). For him, as always, the Gospel he preached was the Gospel that he lived. His food, he said, was *"not to do my own will, but the will of the one who sent me"* (John 5:30). The price the Father called him to pay on behalf of those he loved was total. He literally became like the grain of wheat that he spoke of in one of his parables. *"I assure you,"* he said, *"unless a grain of wheat fall to the ground and die, it remains only a single grain. But, if it dies, it yields a rich harvest"* (John 12:24). Jesus did exactly that. He died so that new life might begin.

The reality of Calvary is frightening to contemplate. It would be bad enough that a criminal should die such an agonizing death. But to think that an innocent man, a sinless one at that, the very Son of God, should have to be subject to such torture and violence is appalling. Although we know that, by the shedding of his blood on the Cross, and the giving up of his life for us, Jesus has won victory over death, the wonder of what this means must have been lost on those who witnessed the sight that Sabbath eve. Calvary was an ugly scene.

In fact, most of Jesus' followers couldn't face it and were long gone. Fearing for their own lives, *"all the disciples deserted him and ran away"* (Matt 26:56). Only a brave and faithful few stood by him at the Cross. Among those were his mother. *"Near the Cross of Jesus was his mother"* (John 19:25).

The sword that Simeon foresaw was now striking without mercy. The Gospel does not credit Mary with a single word at the Cross. Perhaps her grief and anguish did not allow her to speak.

Jesus underwent his agony. He fulfilled his Father's will to the very end. John tells us that, as the final consummation approached, Jesus looked down from the Cross and spoke to Mary and to him. *"Seeing his mother and the disciple he loved standing near her, Jesus said to his mother: 'Woman, this is your son.' Then, to the disciple, he said: 'This is your mother'"* (John 19:26-27).

What are we witness to here? Is it only a case of a son wanting to make sure his mother is taken care of after he's gone? Is it as simple as that?

We would have to wonder why it would be necessary to make such provision for Mary. After all, she did have family. Although we have not yet looked at the question of whether or not she had other children, we would have to assume she surely could have relied on those who are referred to as the brothers and sisters of Jesus to take care of her (Mark 6:3). We don't know much about these people, but we know that the brothers, at least, were well known members of the early Church who were persevering in prayer in the upper room before the coming of the Holy Spirit (Acts 1:14). Surely they would have been more than willing to see to Mary's welfare.

Yet, Jesus confided his mother to John. There is something for us to pursue here.

This is your mother

John, the author of the fourth Gospel, never calls himself, in the text, by his own name. He refers to himself only as *"the disciple whom Jesus loved"* (John 19:26 and many other places). This probably represents a puzzle for most people. How could Jesus love one of his followers more than he loved the others, we might ask?

It's not really such a mystery. We can only love people to the degree that they allow themselves to be loved. John's dedication to Jesus and his commitment to following him was so intense that he probably made himself continually available to his Lord for whatever he might ask him to do. His loyalty was so fierce that he was likely reluctant to leave Jesus' side, no matter what. Everywhere Jesus would turn, there John would be. John was simply allowing himself to be loved. It is difficult not to love a person like that.

I can just see John as the one who wanted always to be nearest to Jesus, whether on the road, at table (witness his position at the Last Supper), or in the market place.

It is not so strange, then, that this 'beloved disciple' was the one who remained with Jesus to the very bitter end. That's loyalty, for sure. It is no wonder Jesus found it so easy to love him.

John was one of the 12, one of the Apostles of the Lamb (Rev 21:14), the foundation stones of the Church Jesus was founding. At Calvary, he was the only one of the 12 present. Judas had gone to his tragic fate, and the others had fled for their lives. Is it out of line, I wonder, to suggest that John was at Calvary, not only as Jesus' loyal friend, but as a representative of the Church? Would it be unusual for Jesus to see him in this light?

I don't think so.

Mary, of course, was at Calvary, too. Towards the end of Jesus' agony, he addresses words to his mother and to John. He assigns them to each other. If John is standing in for the Church, Jesus is appointing his own mother to be mother of the Church, mother, that is, of us all.

From that time on, John writes, *"The disciple took her unto his own"* (John 19:27). Till the end of her life, we are led to assume, Mary's total involvement was with the Church. The only subsequent mention of her is in the Acts of the Apostles, where Luke locates her in the midst of the faithful, in the midst of the Church, in the upper room, persevering in prayer as they all awaited the coming of the Holy Spirit (Acts 1:14). After her removal from this life, do we suppose that her involvement has changed?

The dialogue

We are all familiar with the story. The Lord's messenger was sent to the young woman at Nazareth to announce to her God's amazing plan to save the world by interacting with us in a way we could never have designed or even imagined. The Father would have his own divine Son become one of us, take flesh from a virgin and dwell, pitch his tent, among us. *"The angel Gabriel was sent from God to a town of Galilee called Nazareth, to a virgin betrothed to a man named Joseph, of the house of David. The virgin's name was Mary"* (Luke 1:26-27).

Jesus' conception and birth were miraculous. The power of the Holy Spirit overshadowed Mary, and she conceived. Jesus came into this world by divine power, but at the acquiescence and cooperation of one of us.

Did Mary have to say 'yes'? Obviously not. She was a fully free human being. She could have declined the invitation. Was the entire court of heaven waiting with baited breath, as it were, for her assent? Were the angelic hats thrown in the air when she agreed, when she said: *"Let it be done to me just as you have said"* (Luke 1:38).

The dialogue between Mary and the angel is a fascinating interchange, one that offers intriguing insights to those who look at it with care.

Note that Mary was upset at the manner of Gabriel's greeting. Luke says: *"She was deeply troubled by his words and wondered what his greeting meant"* (Luke 1:29). But he does not say that she was frightened simply by seeing the angel.

Contrast this with what the evangelist says previously about Zechariah's reaction. *"Zechariah was deeply disturbed upon seeing him and was overcome by fear"* (Luke 1:12). I would imagine we would all have somewhat the same reaction. But not Mary. It was what the angel said that bothered her. Is there something here for us to ponder?

Why would she not have been afraid? How about the possibility that she had seen the angel before? Could the Lord have sent the heavenly messenger a number of times to reveal his plan gradually?

Luke's account has it that the message the angel brought to the young woman was that she would bear a child. In the light of her fast-approaching marriage, we would not expect this to surprise her. And yet she seemed puzzled. She had a question for him. How could she conceive a child, she asked him, since she was a virgin? Does this not seem a very unlikely question for a young woman about to be married? It does, for sure.

What does it mean, then? Mary says: *"I am a virgin"* (Luke

1:34). The Greek tense that the sacred writer uses, we are told, implies an ongoing state. It means the same thing as I would mean if I said: "I am a Canadian." The problem Mary was having with the angel's word was, we can speculate, that her promise to the Lord of life-long virginity precluded the possibility of ever having a child at all. Gabriel's explanation of the Holy Spirit's role cleared the whole thing up for her. Her question was entirely acceptable in the eyes of the Lord.

My theory is (and it's only a theory, of course) that the Blessed Mother had had previous visitations from the angel. Let's say three. The first was to call her to devote her life to the Lord. The second was to ask her to accept the Lord's invitation to perpetual virginity for the sake of the kingdom. And the third was to propose a virginal marriage with Joseph, the carpenter, the just man.

Then came the visit that Luke records, announcing something new and unexpected: a child. If this theory be in line with what really happened, I think we can see why Mary reacted the way she did. How can it be that the Lord wishes me to bear a child, she might have asked, since he has already asked the two of us to embrace a life-long virginity? And, in the light of that virginity, how can it happen? These would have been very normal and expected questions. We get the impression that the angel was anticipating her queries because, without breaking stride, he goes on to provide her with the answers she needs.

What about Joseph, we might ask? Did he enter into espousal with Mary without knowing God's plan? Or was he prepared for it? My assumption is that the Lord gave just as much attention to getting him ready as he did to the preparation of Mary herself. How might it have been done? How about dreams? We know from Matthew's Gospel (Matt 1:20, 2:13, 2:19) that, by the time the child had been conceived, Joseph was familiar enough with hearing from the Lord in his dreams.

What about the hesitation Matthew speaks of, describing

Joseph as reluctant to go ahead with the marriage? I expect it had more to do with his profound sense of unworthiness to raise the child.

Mary and Joseph appear in Scripture to be two people meticulously prepared by God to assume the awesome task he had in mind for them. It would seem only logical that he might have taken them through a gradual process of preparation, giving them different opportunities to say 'yes' to his calls.

The foregoing way of understanding the dialogue between the angel Gabriel and the humble maiden of Nazareth is presented only to make the point that those who hold to the ongoing virginity of Mary just may have more Scriptural justification going for them than, at first glance, it might seem.

It is interesting to note, in this context, that the early Protestant reformers—Martin Luther, John Calvin, and Ulrich Zwingli—all taught that Mary did remain a virgin after the birth of Jesus.

The brothers and sisters

Are we all familiar with the reference to Jesus' family in Mark's Gospel? *"This (Jesus) is the carpenter, surely, the son of Mary, the brother of James and Joses and Jude and Simon? His sisters, too, are they not here with us?"* (Mark 6:3). *"Your mother and brothers and sisters are outside asking for you"* (Mark 6:32).

Again and again, it has been pointed out to me that the Catholic Church is in obvious error, in obvious contradiction to the Scriptures, when it insists on the 'tradition' that Mary remained a virgin life-long. And how can I, I am asked, agree with the position taken by my Church?

I have to confess to being somewhat miffed when people confront me with this issue. I am in total agreement with the Church's position on the matter, but it's the implications in the questions that get to me. Am I being told I don't know the Bible too well, perhaps have never even read the passages? Or is it that, having read them, I simply have not seen the obvious? Or, perhaps I am just too stubborn to admit how wrong I have been?

Does the Catholic Church really not know the Bible? Nor the Orthodox Churches either? Do they not have some reason for holding to Mary's perpetual virginity?

This is surely not one of the foundational teachings of the Church, but I think the teaching has a very sound Scriptural base, nonetheless. The dialogue that Luke records between Gabriel and Mary, when rightly understood, really leaves no room for dispute. Mary, and Joseph as well, were called by God into a life-long virginity. That's it. There simply were no other children. Period.

But who, then, are all these people referred to in Mark's Gospel? Just who are James, Joses, Simon, and Jude? Who are the sisters? We're really not sure. One thing we are sure of, however: although they are called brothers and sisters of Jesus, they are not called in Scripture the children of Mary. Who could they be?

There are different possibilities. Custom was at that time (the same even today in the East) to refer to my aunts, uncles, and their children as my 'brothers and sisters'. So, maybe that's who they were.

Some have suggested they were Joseph's children from a previous marriage. This, however, does not hold up in the light of his perpetual virginity as implied in Luke's account.

The explanation I like is the one that posits them as children of Joseph's deceased brother, adopted into Jesus' own household. Life expectancy was not, in those days, what it is today. Many of the men, especially, died rather young, leaving widows and children, 'orphans', the Bible often calls them. Certainly the biblical injunction to take care of widows and orphans is well familiar to us. It was considered, too, a duty for a man to adopt his brother's orphaned children. My thought is that the people in question were adopted by Joseph and brought up in his house. Their mother, the somewhat mysterious "other Mary" (Matt 27:6), sometimes called

"Mary, the mother of James and Joses" (Matt 27:56), sometimes just *"Mary, the mother of James"* (Mark 16:1), was, no doubt, a member of the household as well. She was certainly a faithful follower of Jesus, being present with his own mother at the Cross (Mark 15:40).

We're not entirely sure how many people made up the famous household at Nazareth. But I, for one, would like to have had a chance to visit.

Magnificat

The angel Gabriel said to Mary: *"Blessed are you among women"* (Luke 1:28). Elizabeth said the exact same thing. *"Blessed are you among women,"* she said, *"and blessed is the fruit of your womb"* (Luke 1:42).

Mary's response took her, at the prompting of the Holy Spirit, into poetic song. *"My soul proclaims,"* she sang, *"the greatness of the Lord"* (Luke 1:46). We sing it yet today and call it by its Latin name, *Magnificat*. As she proceeded, Mary prophesied: *"All generations will call me blessed"* (Luke 1:48).

The prophecy has been fulfilled. Down through the centuries, people have called her blessed. In every age, the word she uttered has come true. We fulfill the prophecy every time we repeat the 'Hail Mary'. It is interesting to note that Luke wrote his Gospel probably between the years 80-85 AD, a couple of generations after Mary spoke the words. Not likely he could have written it if, in fact, she was not, even then, being called blessed.

I, for one, do not want to be part of a generation that falls short in making this prophecy of Scripture an ongoing truth.

Dogmas

Jesus did not teach his disciples everything. He said so himself. There were some things they just weren't yet ready to hear (John 16:12). However, he assured them, these things would all unfold in due time. *"The Holy Spirit,"* he told them, *"whom the Father will send in my name, will teach you all the things you need to know"* (John 14:26). And it appears that this ongoing revelation was not to occur all at once. It would happen in more of a human way, as the need would surface. The pattern was made clear to us, we feel, in Acts 15. The Church had a decision to make. Up to that time, virtually all those who were embracing the Gospel, the 'new way' as it was being commonly called, were Jews. It was assumed that basic Jewish practices, such as circumcision, should be retained. And that's what was happening. As more and more non-Jews came to accept Jesus as the promised Messiah, it became first a question and later a rather hotly debated issue. Should non-Jewish believers be made to adopt the customs, laws, and traditions of the Jews?

A meeting was called in Jerusalem. It has been called by many the 'Council of Jerusalem'. Paul and others came a long distance to take part in the deliberations. They prayed. They sought the guidance of the Holy Spirit. They talked. Luke says the discussion went on and on, *"for a long time"* (Acts 15:7). Most of us have been to meetings of this kind. Finally, they reached a decision. James it was who issued the proclamation. He was the presiding elder in the Church at Jerusalem. "It has been decided," he said, *"by the Holy Spirit and by us ..."* (Acts 15:28). The decisions of Councils and the official teaching authority of the Church (the Magisterium) are known as dogmas.

This is how the Holy Spirit teaches the Church. It has continued to happen this way down through the centuries. When matters of revelation are to be clarified, a consultation takes place. Input is sought from the whole Church. The elders (bishops) are consulted. Sometimes they are called into assembly (a Council). These report on the common belief of Christians, the *sensus fidelium*. All pray. The Holy Spirit is consulted. Often, it takes time, 'a long time'. But, in the end, a decision is made and promulgated.

This has happened a few times in matters concerning the Blessed Virgin Mary. The Council of Ephesus (431) had something to say about her. Jesus Christ was true God and true man. And his mother could truly be called the 'God-bearer', in Greek Theotokos. She was rightly to be called the Mother of God for her son was God indeed.

There have been a couple of more recent declarations of the Magisterium about the Blessed Mother which have caused, and continue to cause, considerable discussion among Christians of many denominations. These are the Immaculate Conception (1854) and the Assumption (1950).

These were not new beliefs. The Catholic Church did not, all of a sudden, begin to believe that Mary was conceived without stain of original sin or was assumed body and soul into heaven. These truths had been taking root gradually in the hearts of believers for centuries as the Holy Spirit prompted. But, there came a time when it was deemed fitting that these teachings should be declared official. And so they were.

Do we wonder, perhaps, why the Church believes and teaches such things as the Immaculate Conception and the Assumption? The Church has always taught that public revelation ended with the Son and that anything that developed later must have been contained, at least in seed form, in the original deposit of divine truth. How possibly can the above notions be justified then?

How about Scripture? When the Lord addressed Satan at the very beginning, right after the fall, He said: *"I will place enmity between you and the woman, between your seed and hers. You will lie in wait for his heel, and he will crush your head"* (Gen 3:15). The conqueror of Satan is obviously to be Jesus. The woman is just as obviously Mary. There was to be 'enmity' between her and Satan. The Catholic Church has held that this means Satan would have no hold over her whatsoever. That means no sin. None at all. Immaculately conceived. Not as a reward, of course, for anything she would do. Rather, to prepare a place for the divine Son of God, the one who could never dwell in sin.

And if she is conceived without sin, does it not follow that she would be free from the effects of sin? The final and most devastating effect of sin, of course, is death (Rom 6:23). But if Mary has no sin, how is she to die? The Church has believed, therefore, from way back into the early centuries, that the Blessed Mother did not die, but that she was transfigured, as all believers will be when Jesus returns, and taken to heaven in glory. She experiences now what we will experience later. With her son, Jesus, she is present in glory now before the throne of the Father.

The dogmas we refer to are not new. They are very old. They have resided within the heart of the Church for a long, long time.

A Prophet for today

A more recent development has been catching our attention. Mary is reportedly appearing to people. It is not so much the phenomenon that is new. It is the frequency.

The Church has been slow to approve apparitions. And rightly so. Only a few have received approbation. And these have been declared only 'worthy of belief', not things we must acknowledge. Many, in fact, have been spurious. There are some real horror stories attached to some alleged visions, ones that have developed along cult-like lines and have taken people's focus off the Gospel. These have given all reported apparitions a bad name. Leave it to the enemy to imitate the work of God and try to mess it up.

But some bear the marks of authenticity. Without getting hung up on any one apparition, we have something to learn, I believe, from what's happening.

The message of those that are approved, and those that probably will be, are, as we would suspect, remarkably similar. Mankind, we are told, has been slipping farther and farther away from God. The weight of sin has been increasing and is pressing more heavily than ever before upon human society. Society's structures are sagging under the load and in danger of cracking, of breaking down altogether. The only solution, the general message goes on, is repentance, a turning back to God. Believers are urged to pray and fast that many others will come to the Lord.

This is surely prophecy in the finest biblical tradition. Again and again, the Lord sent prophets to his wayward people, prophets who spoke the word of repentance. But the people would not hear his word. And they had to suffer the consequences. Their communities collapsed and disintegrated.

One of Mary's current roles, then, is as prophet to the Lord's people. She reminds them of their sinful condition and bids them turn to the Lord. She never draws attention to herself, but points always to the Lord, to her divine son.

Is there precedent for this, some ask? There doesn't have to be. If she has been taken to glory with her son, she is well able to appear to us. Just as Jesus appeared to his followers after he rose from the dead, so can he do the same thing now. And he has, if we can believe many impressive reports. He is able to do it, not because he is divine, but by virtue of his glorious state. Mary can do this easily. All she needs is the go-ahead signal from the Father.

St. Thomas Aquinas, still regarded as one of the Church's theologians of pre-eminence, has said that God sends prophets to his Church in every age. It appears that our time is no exception.

A gift from God

Mary, to me, is in a special class. She is that extra something that God gives to people to whom he has already given everything. We have only to accept the gift.

A lot of people struggle with this. They just can't get their heads around it. But it's not a gift for the head. It's a gift for the heart.

Mary is the mother of our Saviour. She was prepared with exquisite care for her role. She is a model for us without parallel in how to respond to God. She followed to the letter the promptings of the Holy Spirit and ministered in her day. She was given by Jesus, her Son, almost with his dying breath, to John who represented, we believe, the whole Church. She was taken up into glory and has continued to follow the Lord's directions as he has directed her to minister to his people, even to being a prophet in our own day.

She is mother of the Church. Like any mother, one of the things she does best, when we let her, is keep us together, with our eyes focussed upon Jesus. She is a gift from God. She is intended by him to be a factor of unity for the whole Body of Christ on earth. Can we look to the time when every quarter of the Church will accept the gift? Speed the day!

Fr. Bob Bedard, CC
Courageous pioneer in the New Evangelization and Parish Renewal

Fr. Bob Bedard (1929-2011) was the Founder of the Companions of the Cross. He came from humble beginnings in Ottawa where he was raised, went to school and was ordained a priest in 1955. He was a high school teacher for many years. Through his involvement in the Charismatic Renewal, the Lord transformed his ministry to his students and as a result many were evangelized and returned to their faith. His extensive speaking at conferences about the renewal of parishes had a tremendous impact and helped numerous people allow the Holy Spirit to be active in their lives. His open and surrendered approach to his faith throughout his life enabled him to say "yes", when the Lord asked for his permission to begin a new community of priests and seminarians in 1985.

In May of 2003 Archbishop Gervais issued the decree establishing the Companions of the Cross as a Society of Apostolic Life. In June of that same year the Servants of the Cross, a group of Sisters following the spirituality of the Companions of the Cross was begun.

The Companions of the Cross have foundations in Ottawa, Toronto, Halifax, Houston and Detroit.

For more information on our books, resources and Lay Formation programs, please visit: **companionscross.org**

A dynamic website with inspiring new content every day!

Sign up for our *'Best of the Web'* email and subscribe to *Gaudium*—A magazine for the New Evangelization.

COMPANIONS OF THE CROSS

We are a community of Catholic priests and seminarians inviting people to know Jesus and empowering them to share Jesus.

> "I see the Church waking up and coming explosively alive to the point where it, with the power of the Holy Spirit, will shake the earth and the nations with its dynamic presence." —Fr. Bob Bedard, CC

Our priests preach the Word of God with passion, celebrate the sacraments with devotion, and lead with confidence.

As Companions of the Cross we root ourselves in:

Brotherhood
A LIFE OF TRUE BROTHERHOOD
We base ourselves on the model of Jesus and his disciples, who lived together, ministered together, and supported one another.

Spirituality
A SPIRITUALITY OF GOD'S POWER AND WISDOM
Jesus's death on the cross and resurrection saved the world. Therefore, we fully commit ourselves to him; seek his will in all we do; and trust in his power to carry it out.

Mission
A MISSION OF EVANGELIZATION AND RENEWAL
We invite all people into an initial and ongoing encounter with Jesus. As we are transformed by his love, we bring about authentic renewal in the Church and the world.

Follow Us:

199 Bayswater Avenue, Ottawa, ON Canada K1Y 2G5 | 1.866.885.8824
info@companionscross.org | WWW.COMPANIONSCROSS.ORG

Made in the USA
Coppell, TX
02 November 2022

85654627R00116